Paper Buying Primer

by Lawrence A. Wilson

GATF*Press*
Pittsburgh

International Standard Book Number: 0-88362-311-0
Library of Congress Catalog Card Number: 2001132469

Printed in the United States of America
Catalog No. 1711
First Edition
July 2001

Printed on Nekoosa Solutions® Recycled White 60-lb. Smooth Text from Georgia-Pacific.

GATF*Press* books are widely used by companies, associations, and schools for training, marketing, and resale. Quantity discounts are available by contacting Peter Oresick at 800/910-GATF.

GATF*Press*
Graphic Arts Technical Foundation
200 Deer Run Road
Sewickley, PA 15143-2600
Phone: 412/741-6860
Fax: 412/741-2311
Email: info@gatf.org
Internet: www.gatf.org • www.gain.net

Orders to:
GATF Orders
P.O. Box 1020
Sewickley, PA 15143-1020
Phone (U.S.): 800/662-3916
Phone (Canada): 613/236-7208
Phone (all other countries): 412/741-5733
Fax: 412/741-0609
Online: www.gain.net

TABLE OF CONTENTS

FOREWORD

Paper is the most expensive material used in the printing plant, so selecting the best paper for a printing job is crucial. Buying paper can be as easy as visiting your local office supply store or calling a paper merchant. But with the immense number of grades available alone, the challenge comes in knowing what and how much you need. From color, weight, and texture to design, printing process, and end use, a number of details must be considered to successfully meet end use requirements, production requirements, customer expectations, and economic price breaks. In eleven chapters, this easy-to-follow primer will help you to make wise and informed decisions in your paper purchase.

The aim of the GATF*Press* primer series is to communicate the essential concepts of printing processes and technologies. Other primers focus on computer-to-plate, lithography, flexography, gravure, on-demand, digital, and screen printing, and new titles are being planned.

Paper Buying Primer is useful to students, graphic artists, print buyers, publishers, salespeople in the graphic communications industry—to anyone who would like to know more about the printing process.

GATF*Press* is committed to serving the graphic communications community as a leading publisher of technical information. Please visit the GATF website at *www.gatf.org* or *www.gain.net* for additional information about our resources and services.

Peter Oresick
Director
GATF*Press*

PREFACE

Buying any product requires a certain level of knowledge about the purpose for which the product is being purchased, the availability of the product, and the cost. Suppose, for example, the purchase of a vehicle was being considered. The term *vehicle* includes such products as trucks, cars, and buses. Or suppose the purchase was a basket of fruit. *Fruit* includes pears, apples, peaches, oranges, and many others. To buy the right fruit or vehicle one needs to know, among other things, what it is going to be used for, any personal preferences, the quality, and the cost. *Paper* is a broad term like *vehicle* and *fruit*.

The buyer who purchases the right product for the job at the best price is one who is knowledgeable about the product lines. This knowledge comes from experience and from resources such as paper merchants, office supply houses, paper mills, and trade organizations. After 30 years in the paper and printing business, however, I have discovered that most buyers don't take full advantage of the available resources. This primer is designed to facilitate communication between buyers and sellers of paper to create a win/win transaction.

Lawrence A. Wilson
Arrowsic, Maine
May 2001

ACKNOWLEDGMENTS

I would like to thank GATF's Peter Oresick and his students at Carnegie Mellon University for the editorial services they contributed to this project as a part of the course "Publishing in the Information Age" during the Spring 2001 semester.

Eric Barker
Adrian Benvenuti
Darren Wai-loon Chan
Han Cheung
Sanjay Dilawari
Ray Hwang
Charles Lan
Wilson Lau
Harry Leitzell
Shraddha Mishra
Stephanie Pflaum
Franklin Szeto
Yuan Qiong Wang
Tony Wu

INTRODUCTION

Buying paper is not difficult. It should be as simple as going to the local office supply house and selecting what you need, or calling a local paper merchant and placing an order. The difficulty arises when paper buyers don't understand the procedures and terminology used by paper suppliers and distributors. Orders that are placed with missing, wrong, or ambiguous information leads to incomplete orders; wrong sizes, weights, or finishes; and missed delivery dates. A paper buyer should be knowledgeable in many areas, including the end-use requirements for the paper and which grade of paper meets those requirements, whether the desired grade is stocked and available, or if a making order is required. Paper ordering consists of many details that need to be included if problems are to be averted.

Fortunately, there is a wealth of information available concerning those details. Mill representatives, merchant salespersons, publications such as mill and merchants catalogs, and trade organization publications such as *What the Printer Should Know About Paper* (GATF*Press)* and *The Paper Buyers' Encyclopedia* (Grade Finders, Inc.) are all excellent sources of information about paper characteristics, various grades, merchant stock, and manufacturer's product lines. *The Paper Buyers' Encyclopedia,* for example, lists over 1,000 grades of paper each designed to meet certain functional requirements for a particular end-use.

Paper buyers will buy paper from office supply houses, paper merchants, or direct from paper mills. Office supply houses sell papers to businesses and homes for use in copiers and inkjet printers.

They also sell specialty papers such as smooth glossy papers for printing quality color reproductions, or gummed label paper. Paper merchants, on the other hand, serve the printing industry as well as businesses and stock a wider variety of papers. Paper is usually ordered directly from the manufacturer if the order is large, or if it must be made to order.

Paper is designed and manufactured for various end-uses: books, newspapers, envelopes, cards, cardboard, covers, and magazines, to name a few. Papers are also designed for printing processes such as offset, letterpress, gravure, laser copiers, and inkjet printers. Ordering the proper paper for a specific job requires knowledge of the end-use requirements and a reliable source of information about the papers that are available to meet those requirements.

The amount of paper required for a given job depends on several factors including number of copies, overrun requirements, amount of trim needed, and handling waste. The most economical use of paper starts with the planning and design stage. A design that requires a non-standard size will require either a making order or excess trimming of a larger sheet. Either choice may significantly increase paper cost. Standard sizes and weights should always be a designer's first consideration.

The number of copies, of course, determines the minimum amount of paper required. The additional amount required depends on the efficiency of the printing and converting operations, and the complexity of the product design. A product that has multiple folds, diecutting, and narrow limits on register and color variation will require more paper for press and folder set-up. One of the most expensive mistakes that can occur in production is to run out of paper before the job is completed and have to pull the job while waiting for more. It is the buyer's responsibility to know how much paper is needed to do any given job and order accordingly.

Another waste of time and paper is ordering paper that is the wrong size. This usually happens when trim, press gripper margins, space for color bars, or grain direction are not taken into account. It is always advisable to check with the pressroom to determine how much space is required for these things. The normal allowance for trim is ⅛ in. and gripper allowance is between ⅜ and ½ in. Depending on the press, color bars usually require ½ in.

The responsibility of the paper buyer is to adequately identify the paper that is being ordered. Is it to be white, green, red, blue, cream white, blue-white, or neutral? Does it have to be thin as an onion skin or as thick as cardboard? Should it be smooth and glossy, smooth and dull, rough or embossed? How thick must it be—how many pages per inch? Does it have to be tear-resistant or fold easily, and will it withstand high web oven temperatures without blistering or becoming too brittle to fold? Paper is readily available to meet all these and other requirements. Knowing what paper is needed by the end-use requirements, how to write the specifications, and the paper's suppliers and availability are all the responsibility of the paper buyer. The more that person knows about buying paper, the more likely the paper ordered will meet production requirements and customer expectations at the lowest possible price.

1 PREPARING TO WRITE AN ORDER

Paper orders should specify size, weight, quantity, grade, caliper, color, grain, finish, brightness, and opacity. Clear specifications accompanying an order will help insure that the appropriate paper for a specific end-use requirement will be received. Part of the challenge in specifying and ordering paper is knowing and using the appropriate terms, including standard size, basic size, basis weight, and grammage.

SIZE

Printing papers are manufactured in large parent rolls and cut into sheets for sheetfed printing or smaller rolls for web presses. **Standard size** refers to full-size sheets of a particular grade line and represents the sizes most commonly used. **Basic size** is the one size among the standard sizes used to establish basis weight. Standard sizes that are stocked may vary from mill to mill, and between merchants. It is advisable to check the availability of sizes and weights with local merchants before committing to a specific sheet size and weight. This will avoid ordering a size that is not stocked, which can lead to an increase in price and delivery time.

WEIGHT

Weight is normally considered to be the actual scale reading for an object, such as the weight of a car, a person, or a bushel of apples. The weight of paper, on the other hand, is a bit more complicated. Paper of course has an actual weight, but there is also what is referred to as **basis weight.**

The actual weight is the weight of a given quantity of paper. A ream is a count designation for 500 sheets, and **ream weight** is the weight, in pounds, of one ream of paper. **"M" weight** is similar to ream weight except it represents 1000 sheets, or twice that of a ream.

Basis weight, however, is the weight, in pounds, of one ream of paper cut to its basic size. Basis weight, while an actual weight under a certain condition, is really a descriptive term. The only time basis weight is an actual weight is when 500 sheets of the grade's basic size is weighed. For example, the basis weight and actual weight for book paper are the same only when 500 sheets size 25×38 in. (635×965 mm)—the grade's basic size—are weighed. If 500 sheets of 25×38-in. book paper weigh 50 lb., then both the basis weight and the actual weight are 50 lb.

Internationally, the weight of all paper and paperboard is expressed as **grammage,** which is the weight in grams of one single sheet of paper whose area is one square meter (39.37×39.37 in.). When the basic weights of papers, as used in the United States, are converted to grammage, their common denominator or weight relationship becomes readily apparent. For example, a 20-lb. bond

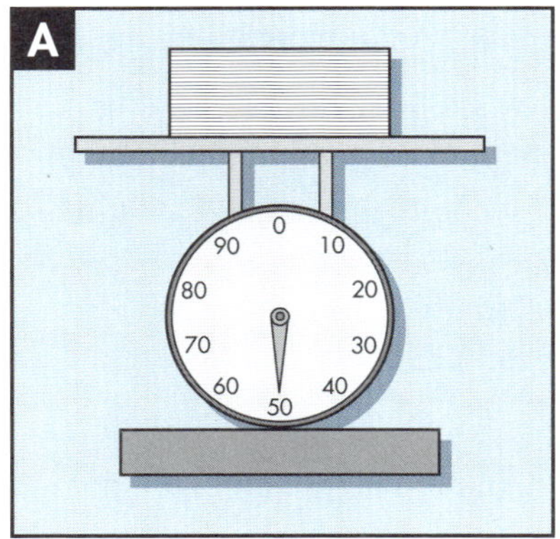

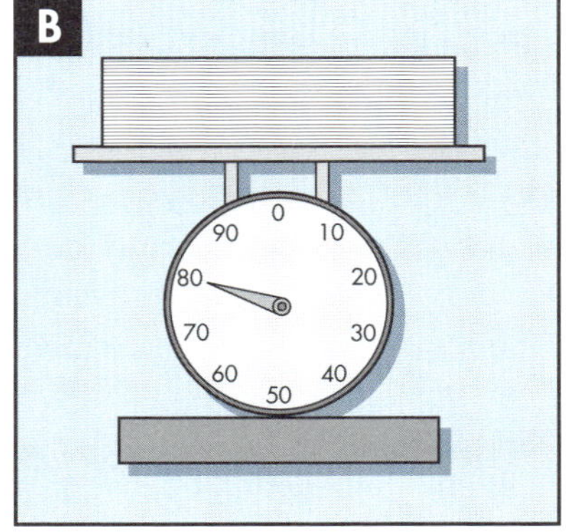

Illustration A shows that 500 sheets of 25×38-in. book paper (the basic size for book paper) weigh 50 lb. In other words, the basis weight and the actual weight are the same. If the same stock is cut into larger sheets, a ream will weigh more. In illustration B, the stock is still a 50-lb. stock, but the actual weight per ream is now 80 lb.

and a 50-lb. book paper have respective grammages of 75 and 74 g/m² or nearly, but not exactly, the same weight.

Designers, printers, and customers will specify a desired paper as a 50-lb. book paper, or a 24-lb. bond paper. These are descriptive terms that describe the characteristics of paper. An 80-lb. book paper, for example, is thicker, more opaque, and stiffer than a 50-lb. book paper. If the ordered size of the book paper is 25×38 in. (basic sheet size), then 500 sheets will weigh 50 lb. However, if the ordered size is anything other than 25×38 in., then the actual weight must be calculated.

Grade	Basic Size
Coated offset, book, label	25×38 in. (635×965 mm)
Coated cover	20×26 in. (508×660 mm)
Bond, business, duplicator, copy	17×22 in. (432×559 mm)
Vellum bristol	22½×28½ in. (572×724 mm)
Index	25½×30½ in. (648×775 mm)
Tag	24×36 in. (610×914 mm)

Paper grade lines and their respective basic sheet size.

Calculating Weight

The actual weight of any sheet within a given grade line that is larger or smaller than the basic size sheet can be determined by dividing the area of this new sheet by the area of the basic size sheet; this number is then multiplied by the basis weight, as shown in the following formula:

$$\text{Actual weight} = \frac{\text{Area of new sheet}}{\text{Area of basic size sheet}} \times \text{Basis weight}$$

Here is an example using a 35×45-in. sheet of 50-lb. book paper, which has a basic size of 25×38 in.

$$\text{Actual weight} = \frac{35 \text{ in.} \times 45 \text{ in.}}{25 \text{ in.} \times 38 \text{ in.}} \times 50 \text{ lb.}$$

$$= \frac{1{,}575 \text{ sq. in.}}{950 \text{ sq. in.}} \times 50 \text{ lb.}$$

$$= 1.658 \times 50 \text{ lb.}$$

$$= 82.9 \text{ lb.}$$

In this example, the 35×45-in. sheet is 1.658 times larger than the 25×38-in. sheet. Therefore, the weight of the 35×45-in. sheet is also 1.658 times heavier than the 25×38-in. sheet. The actual ream weight of the 35×45-in. sheet of 50-lb. book paper would be 82.9 lb. The "M" weight would be twice the ream weight (82.9 lb. × 2 = 165.8 lb.).

Basic Size (inches)	**Single-sheet area** (sq. in.)	**500-sheet ream area** (sq. ft.)	**Papers**
17×22	374	1,299	Bond, business, duplicator, copy
20×26	520	1,806	Cover
22½×28½	641	2,227	Vellum bristol
25½×30½	778	2,700	Index
24×36	864	3,000	Tag
25×38	950	3,300	Coated offset, book, label

Single-sheet and 500-sheet ream area for several basic sizes of paper.

Another method for calculating weight uses a "constant factor" chart. The chart for book paper, adapted from *The Paper Buyers' Encyclopedia,* is shown on the facing page. First find the number of square inches in your proposed size, then multiply the number of square inches by the constant factor for the basis weight of the paper being used. This gives the weight of 1,000 sheets.

For example, the size ordered is 46×58 in. with a basis weight of 80 lb. Multiply 46 by 58 to get the number of square inches, 2,668. Under the chart heading "Basis weight" find 80 lb. and its corresponding constant factor of 0.1684. Multiply 2,668 by 0.1684, which equals 449 lb. This calculation determines that 1,000 sheets of a 46×58 basis 80 paper weighs 449 lb.

Basis Weight	1,000-Sheet Factor (Constant Factor)
25	0.0526
30	0.0632
35	0.0737
40	0.0842
45	0.0947
50	0.1053
55	0.1158
60	0.1263
65	0.1368
70	0.1474
75	0.1579
80	0.1684
85	0.1789
90	0.1895
95	0.2000
100	0.2105
120	0.2526
140	0.2947
150	0.3158

Constant factors for calculating the weight of sheets of book paper at other than its basic size of 25×38 in. (Adapted from The Paper Buyers' Encyclopedia)

A grade line consists of not only various sizes, but also various basis weights. Book papers, for example, range from a basis of 30 lb. up to 150 lb., while label papers range from 30 lb. up to 100 lb.

HOW TO DETERMINE EQUIVALENT WEIGHTS

Equivalent weight is a system of comparing papers of different basic sheet sizes and basis weights. Equivalent weights are used to compare the weight of two grades with different basic sizes. For example, what weight of book paper would be equivalent to a 24-lb. bond. This determination is usually made using a reference table. In the following chart, from *What the Printer Should Know About Paper*, note that a bond paper with a basis weight of 24 lb. is roughly

Type of Paper	Book (25×38)	Bond (17×22)	Cover (20×26)	Bristol (22½×28½)	Index (25½×30½)	Tag (24×36)
Book	**30**	12	16	20	25	27
	40	16	22	27	33	36
	45	18	25	30	37	41
	50	20	27	34	41	45
	60	24	33	40	49	55
	70	28	38	47	57	64
	80	31	44	54	65	73
	90	35	49	60	74	82
	100	39	55	67	82	91
	120	47	66	80	98	109
Bond	33	**13**	18	22	27	30
	41	**16**	22	27	33	37
	51	**20**	28	34	42	46
	61	**24**	33	41	50	56
	71	**28**	39	48	58	64
	81	**32**	45	55	67	74
	91	**36**	50	62	75	83
	102	**40**	56	69	83	93
Cover	91	36	**50**	62	75	82
	110	43	**60**	74	90	100
	119	47	**65**	80	97	108
	146	58	**80**	99	120	134
	164	65	**90**	111	135	149
	183	72	**100**	124	150	166
Bristol	100	39	54	**67**	81	91
	120	47	65	**80**	98	109
	148	58	81	**100**	121	135
	176	70	97	**120**	146	162
	207	82	114	**140**	170	189
	237	93	130	**160**	194	216
Index	110	43	60	74	**90**	100
	135	53	74	91	**110**	122
	170	67	93	115	**140**	156
	208	82	114	140	**170**	189
Tag	110	43	60	74	90	**100**
	137	54	75	93	113	**125**
	165	65	90	111	135	**150**
	192	76	105	130	158	**175**
	220	87	120	148	180	**200**
	275	109	151	186	225	**250**

Equivalent ream weights for different types of paper. Basic weights are in **bold** *type. (From* What the Printer Should Know about Paper*)* equivalent to a book paper with a basis weight of 61 lb. Book paper with a basis weight of 60 lb. could be substituted for 24-lb. bond, in some cases, because they are roughly equivalent in weight. The bulk, however, may be different. The bold figures in the chart indicate the available basis weights, and the light figures are the equivalent basis weights in different papers. All weights shown are for 500-sheet reams.

Each grade line contains a range of sizes and basis weights. Book papers, for example, have twenty-five standard sizes ranging from 17½×22½ in. up to 52×76 in. Each size is available in twelve different basis weights ranging from 30 lb. up to 150 lb. It is important to remember that each grade has its own basic sheet size and basis weight.

Basis weight influences other physical properties of paper such as caliper, stiffness, opacity, and folding. Paper with a basis weight of 30 will have less caliper, be less stiff, and have less opacity than the same paper at a basis weight of 60. A thin lightweight paper folds more easily and has less tendency to crack at the fold than a thicker, heavier-weight paper.

CALIPER

While there is a relationship between caliper and basis weight, there are exceptions. A finishing operation such as supercalendering will compact the sheet, causing the caliper to decrease while weight remains unchanged. This makes it possible for a 60-lb. sheet to have the same or smaller caliper than a lighter-weight sheet. This is why it is important to understand what a grade line means. A 60-lb. supercalendered glossy coated book paper is one grade, while a 60-lb. matte finished book paper is another grade. Both use 25×38 in. as their basic sheet size but 60-lb. supercalendered glossy paper will be thinner than 60-lb. matte paper—even though they both weigh 60 lb.

Caliper can be used to estimate the weight of a given paper within the same grade line. Caliper is measured by means of a micrometer and reported in thousandths of an inch, or points (pt.).

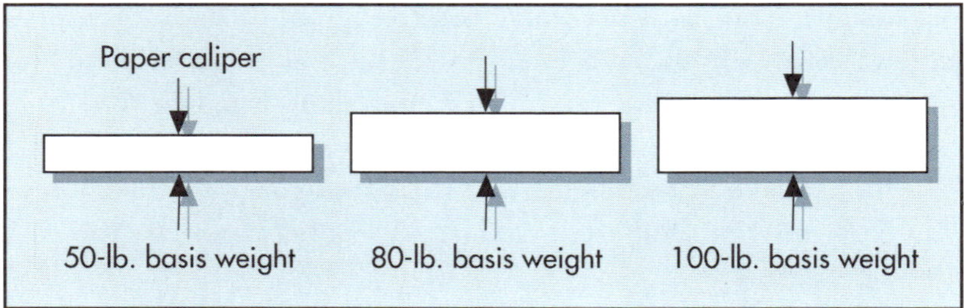

An increase in basis weight generally increases the caliper, or thickness, of the sheet.

One point is equal to one thousandth of an inch (0.001 in., or 0.025 mm). A coated glossy book paper, basis weight of 50, will caliper approximately 0.0025 in. (0.064 mm) while a basis 80 coated glossy will caliper approximately 0.004 in. (0.102 mm). Regular finish offset, basis weight 50, has a caliper of 0.004 in., or 4 points, while basis 70 has a caliper of 0.005 in.

COLOR

The concept of color is both fascinating and sometimes confusing. Light is considered additive. In other words, beams of colored light, when added, will create another color. White, for example, is the combination of equal parts red, green, and blue light, which are the primary colors of the spectrum. It takes a bit of mental adjustment to look at a white sheet of paper and visualize a combination of red, green, and blue reflected light producing the white surface. Reflected light from a white paper surface can be passed through a prism to illustrate this point. The prism separates the "white light" into a spectrum of colors: red, orange, yellow, green, blue, indigo, and violet. A surface such as paper will take on the color of the light that is shining upon it. It can only reflect the colors present in the light that is illuminating its surface. Paper that has the ability to reflect equal parts of red, green, and blue light will be seen as white when all three colors are equally present. However, if the light shining on the paper is red alone, then the paper will be seen as red.

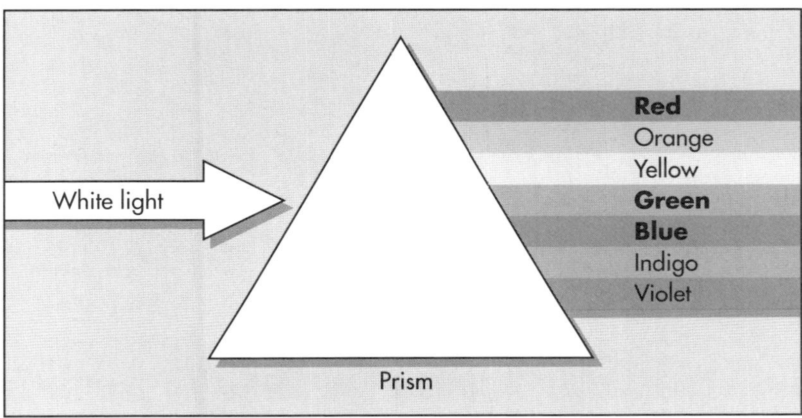

White light, when passed through a prism, is separated into a spectrum of color. The primary colors of white light are red, blue, and green.

While light sources are considered additive, filters, on the other hand, subtract colors. If a white surface is viewed through a green filter, the result is a green color because the filter allows only the green light to pass, filtering out the red and blue. White paper is generally used for four-color printing because white paper has the ability to reflect red, green, and blue light. The inks used for four-color process printing modify the light reflected from the paper's surface because transparent inks are filters.

A set of four-color process inks consists of cyan, magenta, yellow, and black inks. Cyan is blue-green and absorbs red light. Magenta is blue-red and absorbs green light, while yellow absorbs blue light. An overprint of cyan, magenta, and yellow should produce black because the three inks are absorbers for the primary colors of red, blue, and green. However, the pigments in cyan, magenta, and yellow inks are not perfect, and they do not absorb 100% of the reflected light and the overprint appears brownish-black. Therefore, black ink is used to reinforce shadow areas that call for true black.

Paper that is used for four-color process work should reflect high levels and equal amounts of blue, green, and red light in order to produce accurate colors. However, white paper comes in

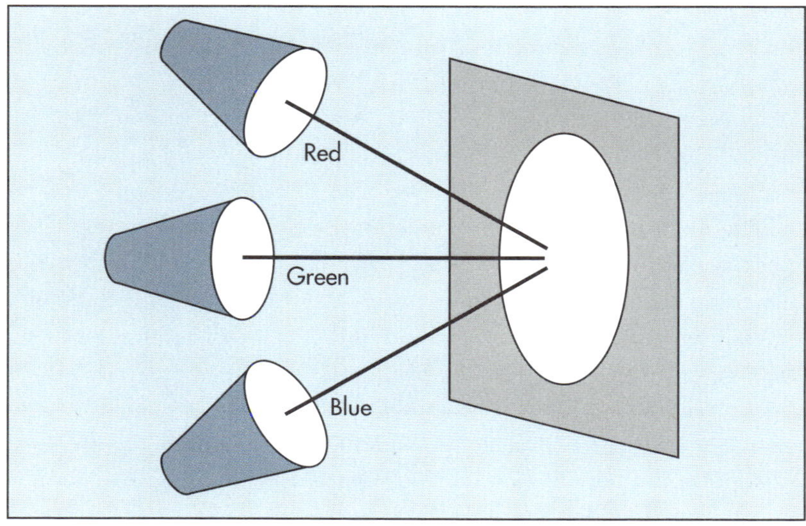

With additive color, red, green, and blue light, when added, produce white.

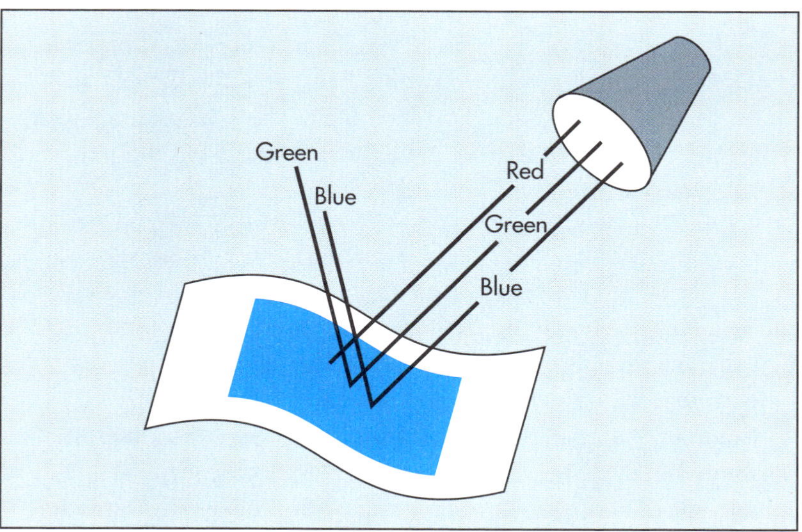

With subtractive color, a transparent ink film functions as a filter. When white light (red, green, and blue light) shines on a film of cyan ink, the blue and green light waves pass through the transparent film, and reflect from the paper's surface to pass back through the film to the eye of the observer. The red light waves, however, are absorbed by the cyan ink film.

many different shades, ranging from blue-white to cream-white. If the reflected light from paper is higher in red, the paper appears cream or warm in color and is referred to as cream-white. If the paper reflects a higher amount of blue, the paper is called blue-white. While the shade can affect tonal reproduction, such as skin tones, shade is usually chosen for aesthetic considerations.

The materials from which paper is made, the fibers and pigment, are naturally a warm white. Using the brightest pigments and bleaching the fibers to the maximum whiteness will produce a sheet that is bright and on the warm white side. Producing a blue-white sheet requires the addition of a blue dye, reducing the amount of red and yellow light that is being reflected and also reducing brightness. The one exception is when fluorescent dyes are used. Most premium papers contain fluorescent dye. These dyes actually absorb ultraviolet light and reflect it as blue light. However, for this to take place the illuminating source must contain ultraviolet light, which most artificial light does not. Shade can change according to the light under which viewing occurs, so it is always advisable to view papers in room light as well as under light that contains ultraviolet light: outdoors or within a viewing booth.

It is easiest for the eye to distinguish differences between papers of different shades when a direct comparison is made. It is therefore important not to mix varying shades within the same printed piece. It is not unusual for this mixing to happen when "equivalent" grades are mixed from various manufacturers. Because shade is a manufacturer's choice, there may be considerable variation between manufacturers. A competitive or equivalent grade may be blue-white from one mill and cream-white from another.

Color attributes are hue, saturation, and brightness. **Hue** is that attribute that describes color as being red, yellow, green, or blue or as some color in between such as red-yellow, or blue-green. **Saturation** is the intensity of the color. The more vivid a color, the higher its saturation. **Brightness** is the attribute that measures the level of emitted or reflected light. A paper that has the ability to reflect a higher level of light is brighter than one that reflects a lower level of light.

DESCRIPTION OF PAPER

Paper orders should carry an adequate description of the paper ordered, such as the manufacturer's brand name along with grade designation and specifications. Each mill uses a unique name to designate a particular brand. Names like Buffalo Gloss, Arrowsic Matte, or Woolwich Dull are created by the manufacturer to identify and market their particular products. Grades, however, are common to all mills. Coated offset, bristol, vellum opaque, liner board, catalog, envelope, and tag are just a few of the grade names. The following chapter will take a closer look at paper grades.

Each paper grade is designed to meet certain requirements. Tag, for example, is a heavy-duty printing paper with strength, rigidity, and a lint-free surface. It is designed for scoring and diecutting, and it gives sharp images by lithography, letterpress, or silk screen. This grade is recommended for, among other things, cards, catalog covers, job tickets, and annual reports. The paper ordered should meet printing and converting requirements, must be suitable for the ink used, and must meet the physical requirement of the job. With so many grades available, the problem is to know what is needed and what is available. Again, an excellent place to start is with a merchant or mill.

GRAIN

Paper grain is a function of fiber orientation and drying stresses, and it runs in the direction that paper travels through the paper machine. Papermakers refer to fiber orientation as being either in the **machine direction** (grain direction) or **cross-machine direction.**

Printers, on the other hand, refer to grain direction as being **grain-short** (cross grain) or **grain-long** (with the grain). Paper is called grain-long if the grain runs parallel to the press cylinders. This usually means the grain runs with the longest dimension of the paper. For example, grain that runs parallel to the 38-in. (965-mm) dimension of a 25×38-in. (635×965-mm) sheet would be grain-long. It would be grain-short paper if the grain ran parallel to the 25-in. (635-mm), or short, direction.

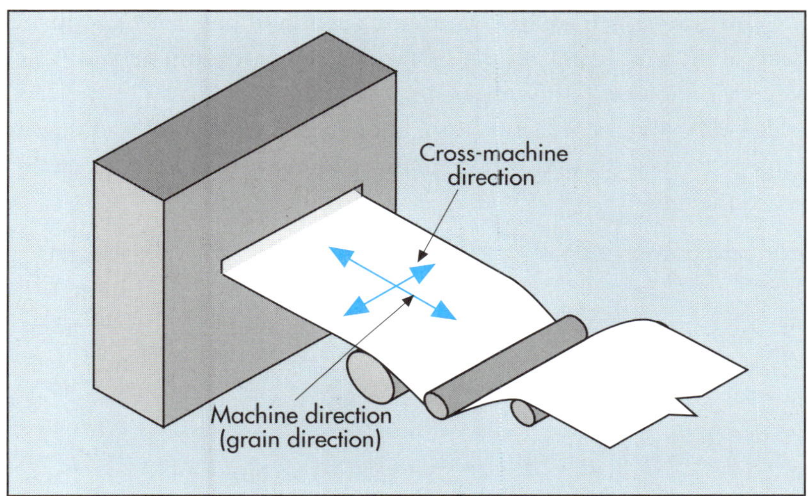

On a papermaking machine the fibers are aligned with the direction that the machine travels. Hence papermakers refer to the fiber orientation, or grain, as being in the machine direction.

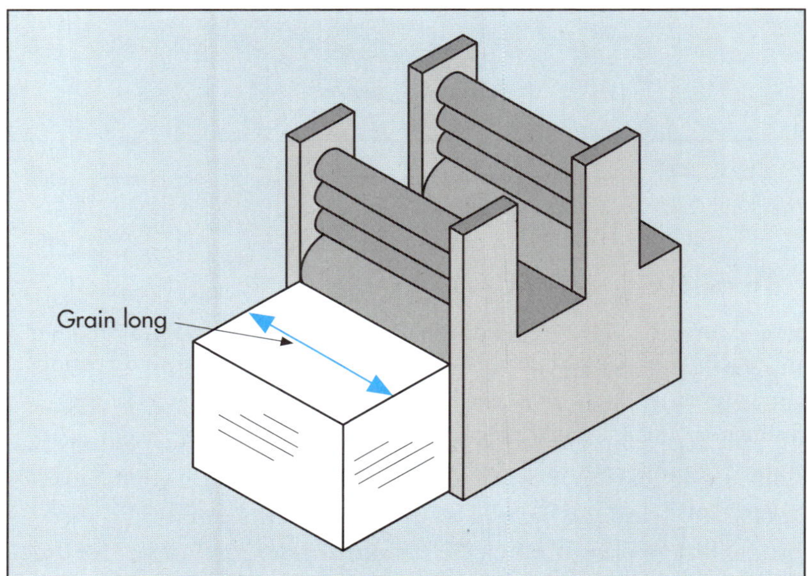

Printers refer to paper grain as being long if it runs parallel with the face of the printing cylinders.

One way to determine the grain direction of paper is to gently place a piece of paper on the surface of water (it is important to keep the top side of the paper dry). As the paper floats on the water, the side in contact with the water will begin to wet and the paper will start to curl. The grain direction of the paper runs parallel to the curl.

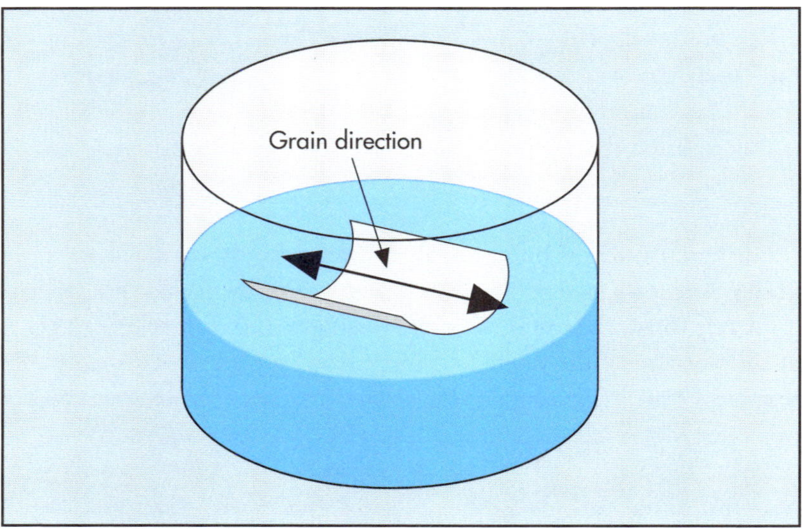

One method for determining paper grain is to float a sample of paper on water. The grain will be parallel to the curl.

FINISH

Paper surfaces may be finished in a variety of ways, ranging from a mirror-like glossy surface to one that is dull and rough or dull and smooth. The choice of finishes depends on the printing process, graphic reproduction requirements, as well as aesthetic considerations. Designers are more likely to choose paper for its feel and appearance, and the paper's aesthetic effect on the finished piece. Production people, on the other hand, are more interested in the way the paper performs on press and in the bindery along with ink holdout and foldability. Letterpress and gravure require a smooth surface for proper ink transfer from the printing cylinder. Process color printing requires a smooth surface, with the ability to hold ink varnishes on the surface while permitting ink solvents to drain into the surface to facilitate ink setting.

The finish on a surface of paper begins with the papermaking process. Through refining, fiber selection, and drying, surfaces can be made rough for antique grades, or smooth for machine finish grades. **Antique** describes a rough surface with maximum bulk-to-weight ratio. Antiques are soft to the touch and are used for bulking and creating an "old" or antique look. **Machine finish** is the designation for a smooth finish that is produced on a paper machine. There are several finishes between antique and machine finish. Each one is designed to meet a particular production requirement such as bulk, ink absorption, or a particular look and feel.

A **felt finish** is produced by embossing a design in the surface at the wet end of the paper machine. This type of finish is used for text, cover, and wedding papers. Other finishes are **wove** and **laid,** both of which are created by special rolls that emboss the paper during the papermaking operation. Finishes can be and usually are imparted into the surface of the paper after it has been made on the paper machine. The post-finishing operation usually requires that the surface be coated. The coating is pliable and responds to a finishing operation better than a fibrous surface. The surface may be finished by a supercalender that imparts a smooth glossy surface. If the calender rolls are micro-roughened, a dull smooth surface will result. Finishes can also be a large embossed pattern that simulates wood grain, snake skin, pebble surface, or other unique patterns.

Paper machine finishes are identified by name: antique, wove, vellum, laid, etc. If the paper is embossed, it is identified by its pattern, number, or name. If there is any doubt, submit a paper sample in the desired finish along with the order. For deckle-edge or laid-finish papers, indicate grain and the direction of the deckled edge or laid lines.

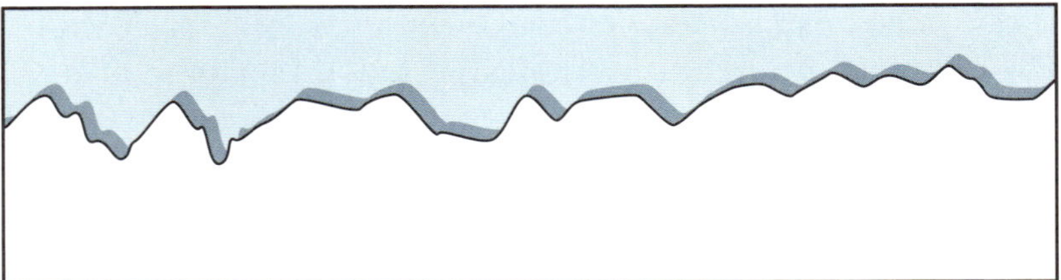

A deckle-edge paper is produced naturally on a paper machine or handmade papers. This edge is normally trimmed off, but is retained when an order calls for a deckle edge.

Printing papers also include cast-coated grades that are coated and dried on highly polished chrome drums producing a mirror-like surface and used for label, covers, and specialty boxes. Coated offset has a surface that is coated and finished either by supercalenders or inline calendering operations on the paper machine. The surface of coated grades can be made at various levels of gloss and brightness depending on the pigment used, thickness of coating, and calendering operation. Gloss is measured on a scale from zero to one hundred, with glossy coated papers, for example, ranging from sixty to the mid-nineties. The products for which coated offset papers are designed range from textbooks to colorful brochures and annual reports.

2 Paper Types

This chapter lists some of the most common paper types. For a comprehensive list of grades see *The Paper Buyers' Encyclopedia,* where over 1,000 different grade names are listed. Another excellent source of information is the merchant's paper catalog and price book.

ADHESIVE-COATED PAPERS

Used primarily for printed labels, adhesive-coated papers have an adhesive that is either activated by water or heat, or is permanently tacky. **Gummed papers,** with water-activated adhesives, have either a conventional or dry type of applied gumming. The dry type of gummed paper is preferred by printers because of its lower tendency to curl over a broader range of relative humidities.

Two essential considerations in selecting a gummed paper are the type of surface desired for printing and the type of gumming that will adhere to the target surface. Gummed papers are made with different adhesive formulations geared to the specific qualities of the target surface. Gummed papers are fabricated with a variety of surfaces and from different types of paper, including uncoated white and colored paper; glassine, glossy-coated, cast-coated, and low-gloss-coated white and colored papers; papers with a metallic surface (such as gold or silver); and foil-mounted paper. When selecting a gummed paper for printed labels, printers should specify the surface to which the labels will be adhered. Since gummed papers are more prone to curl than other papers, extra precaution should be taken to keep them wrapped when not being processed.

Heat-seal papers are coated with an adhesive that becomes tacky when heated. These papers are used for instant and permanent adhesion to surfaces like plastic, glass, and vinyl (phonograph records, for example). Heat-seal papers, because of their high instant tack, are well suited for high-speed packaging. Selection of the proper heat-seal paper involves evaluating the surface to be labeled, the method and machinery to be used, and the dwell time for heat activation. Intense heat, such as that used for drying ink, must be avoided when printing heat-seal papers.

Pressure-sensitive adhesive-coated papers have an adhesive that is permanently tacky at normal temperature and adheres to a surface by contact and applied pressure. Because of their unique properties, adhesive-coated papers require special printing and handling care. Helpful suggestions are available from suppliers of these papers.

BIBLE PAPER

Once printed only by letterpress, Bible papers are the forerunner of lightweight printing papers and have exceptionally high opacity for a lightweight paper. In addition to Bibles, lightweight papers are also used for handbooks, manuals, dictionaries, financial and legal printing, and professional reference books because they reduce bulk and mailing costs. The subsequent savings in postage and distribution realized with lightweight papers can often far outweigh their high initial costs. Special adjustments and techniques are usually required for the efficient handling of lightweight papers during printing. Such information is available from the manufacturer. Web offset, however, has made it easier to print lightweight papers, and a value analysis may reveal substantial savings. Bible papers weigh 17–40 lb./ream (25–59 g/m^2) based on a 25×38-in. (635×965-mm) sheet size.

BLANKS

Blanks are thick types of paperboard produced on a cylinder machine with surfaces designed for printing. Uncoated blanks may be white-lined on one or both sides for printing, while coated blanks are coated on one or both sides. Grain direction is an important consideration relative to the curvature of the press cylinder and to the blank's end-use. Heavier blanks are best handled on presses having large cylinder diameters which reduce excessive bending. Excessive bending and ink tack must be avoided to prevent separation of the plies. Blanks are used for printed signs, point-of-purchase and window display signage, streetcar and bus cards, posters, and calendar backs. The thickness of blanks ranges from 15–48 pt. (0.38–1.22 mm), thickness being determined by the number of plies laid down by the paper machine.

BOND PAPERS

Classified as writing paper, bond papers differ from book or printing papers in several important ways. Bond papers must have permanence; durability for handling, folding, and loose-leaf binding; and adequate internal and surface hardness for pen-and-ink writing, erasure, and typing. Stiffness and rattle are required for letterheads and documents. Some compromises in printing properties, such as reduced opacity and dimensional stability, are made to meet these other end-use requirements. Bond papers are made in various grades. **Utility bond** has no watermark and is made from chemical wood pulp. It is used for printed products like letterheads, invoices, statements, forms, price lists, short-term policies, and direct-mail advertising enclosures. **Watermarked bond,** also an all-chemical wood pulp sheet, is a stronger, brighter, better-quality bond than un-watermarked bond. The basic size for bond papers is 17×22 in. (432×559 mm) with standard basis weights of 13, 16, 20, and 24 lb./ream (49, 60, 75, and 90 g/m^2).

The best bond is a premium-quality, air-dried, cockle-finish, all-chemical-wood bond made by some manufacturers. Next in order of quality and cost are the cotton-content bond papers, formerly designated as *rag content.* Quality levels are watermarked as either 25, 50, 75, or 100% cotton-fiber bond paper, with the watermarked 100% cotton fiber bond being a premium sheet. These grades of bond are formed exceptionally well on slow-running paper machines, and are air-dried for added strength and a cockle finish. Bond papers containing cotton add class and a distinctive character to printed letterheads and documents, and they can be matched with envelopes of equal quality. An erasable type of bond paper allows corrections to be made. Because bond papers have a hard surface, inks must be carefully chosen and special care must be exercised during printing.

Business forms bond is a type of bond paper manufactured for the specific requirements of non-heatset web printing and continuous business forms. In forms printing, both colored and white register bonds are used to differentiate the sheets (plies) in a set of forms. Specific paper requirements for forms printing include rapid ink absorption, adequate strength and stiffness for printing, dimensional stability for registration of collated forms, and a surface capable of accepting clean, sharp carbon impressions. Other requirements include close control of caliper, exceptionally good roll quality, and the ability to be refolded and stacked at high speed for computer printouts. The basic size for business forms bond is 17×22 in. (432×559 mm), with the most common basis weights being 12, 15, 18, and 20 lb./ream (45, 56, 68, and 75 g/m^2).

In addition to business, professional, and personal stationery, high-quality bond papers are used for insurance policies, certificates, statements, deeds, and long-life documents. Some bond paper grades are available in colors, and in finishes such as laid and linen. Some bond papers are designed for uses other than printing.

BRISTOL PAPER

Uncoated printing bristols are made from chemical wood pulp (free of groundwood) in white and colors. Finishes are *smooth* and *vellum.* A vellum-finish bristol is widely used for offset lithography because of its higher bulk, pleasing surface, and ability to set inks quickly with minimum setoff. Because of their excellent strength and bulk, printing bristols are used for cover applications. The basic size for bristol paper is 22½×28½ in. (572×724 mm), with basis weights of 67, 80, 100, 120, 140, and 160 lb./ream (147, 176, 219, 263, 307, and 351 g/m^2).

Index bristols are made with a smooth finish in white and colors, and are available in different grades, including those made from all-chemical wood pulp and 25, 50, or 100% cotton fiber. Because of their toughness, stiffness, good writing and erasing surface, and resistance to repeated handling, index bristols are used for file cards and records, index systems, ruled forms, mailing cards, diecut novelties, and covers. A typical application for cotton-content index bristols is the filing cards used in libraries, institutions, and government agencies. Index bristols have a basic size of 25½×30½ in. (648×775 mm), with basis weights of 90, 110, 140, and 170 lb./ream (163, 199, 253, and 308 g/m^2).

Postal bristols are made specifically for postcard use, in either white or light-cream color. They have a smooth, uniform finish designed for pen-and-ink writing and a caliper suitable for mail-processing equipment.

Coated bristols, used for heavyweight cover applications and for picture postcards, are available with coating on one or both sides and in white and colors. Standard thicknesses are 8, 10, 11, and 12 pt. (0.20, 0.25, 0.28, and 0.30 mm).

CARBONLESS PAPERS

These are replacing many carbon-interleaved paper forms because they simplify paper work, produce smudge-free copies, and eliminate the messiness associated with the use and disposal of carbon paper. Carbonless papers are technically different from regular papers. They incorporate a chemical transfer system and use a reaction between two different chemical coatings to transfer images. The backside of the top sheet in the carbonless set is coated with encapsulated chemicals. The intermediate sheets have a receptor coating on the front side and an encapsulated coating on the back side, with the last sheet of the set having a receptor coating only. When pressure is applied to the top sheet of the set by typing, writing, or "crash printing," an image is formed by the reaction between the chemicals liberated from the collapsed capsules and the contacting receptor coating. Special precaution must be taken not to damage the encapsulated chemicals by excessive pressure and friction during handling, printing, cutting, and trimming. The proper side of each paper used in the set must be printed so that the sheets are collated in their required sequence. Manufacturers of carbonless papers provide specific instructions for the printing and processing of these papers.

COATED PRINTING PAPER

Coated papers, also known as **enamels,** are manufactured for sheetfed offset in various grade levels and designated as 1, 2, 3, 4, or Premium. The finishes of coated papers range from the super high gloss of cast-coated enamels to the "glossless" look of matte coated papers. The basic size for coated printing paper is 25×38 in. (635×965mm), with basis weights of 60, 70, 80, and 100 lb./ream (89, 104, 118, and 148 g/m^2).

Cast-coated paper, whose surface is produced by a casting process, is a special and separate type of paper. This paper has an exceptionally smooth, level surface and a mirror-like gloss. Cast-coated paper bulks higher because it is not supercalendered. It is used for covers, high-quality boxes, and specialty products.

Dull enamels, like high-gloss enamels, are supercalendered but use different coating formulations to produce a dull surface, with a gloss of 25–35. Dull coated enamels are used where good ink hold-out and a smooth lay of ink like that of glossy enamels is desired, but without a glossy paper background. Dull enamels are used for annual reports, catalogs, product brochures, and books, and for printing jobs requiring high-quality multicolor reproduction with minimal paper gloss.

Coated matte grades combine some of the advantages of both uncoated and coated dull papers. While they do not have the high degree of ink holdout that fully coated paper has, their lithographic reproduction is far superior to that of uncoated papers. With a glare-free background and a maximum gloss of 0–20, matte-coated papers handle like uncoated paper on press. They generally have a higher bulk and opacity than enamel papers of the same weight because they are not supercalendered, and have less coating and therefore more fibers. The basic size of coated matte papers is 25×38 in. (635×965 mm), with standard basis weights of 50, 60, 70, 80, and 100 lb./ream (74, 89, 104, 118, and 148 g/m^2).

Embossed enamel papers are available in various embossed patterns. They offer the high reproduction fidelity of a coated paper along with a textured background. These papers are used for specialty products as well as covers and brochures.

Coated web offset papers are made for the specific requirements of a web press and heatset drying, and are available in high-gloss enamel, dull-finish enamel, and matte surfaces. The upper limit of their basis weight, at a basic size of 25×38 in. (635×965 mm), generally does not exceed 100 lb./ream (148 g/m^2) because of blistering in the hot-air dryer during printing, and because of folding considerations.

COVER PAPERS

Cover paper must have sufficient strength and durability to protect its contents under normal use. It may be required to match the color and surface texture of the inside paper or be distinctly different in appearance. Additional requirements may involve diecutting, embossing, varnishing, lacquering, the printing of metallic inks, scoring, stapling, and drilling. **Coated cover papers** are used because of their enhanced print quality and ink holdout. Surfaces may have a glossy or dull finish. Most coated covers match the color and finish of a companion coated paper. Coated covers are available in white and numerous colors, and in different finishes, grades, and basis weights. Colors may be brilliant, bright, pastel, or subdued, depending on the needs of the designer. Finishes include plate, smooth, wove, vellum, laid, and felt, as well as embossed finishes having various patterns. The basic size of cover paper is 20×26 in. (508×660 mm), with basis weights ranging from 50 lb./ream (135 g/m^2) to as high as 19 pt. in thickness (0.48 mm). Cover paper's primary functions are physical and aesthetic.

Laminating two cover papers having a different color or finish makes duplex covers. Coated bristol papers and tag papers often fulfill the strength requirement for a thick, stiff coated cover. Specialty cover papers include plastic-laminated and pyroxylin-coated covers, which are water-, soil-, and grease-resistant, and require special inks for their printing. Other specialty covers are coated with mica, gold, or silver. Their surfaces may be embossed, flocked, or velour-textured. The embossed patterns can resemble the texture of leather or cloth. When creating attractive, functional covers for booklets, annual reports, catalogs, and advertising, graphic designers can choose from a wide variety of attractive and functional cover stocks.

LABEL PAPERS

Coated on one side ("C1S"), these are designed for the diverse requirements of printed label manufacture, application, and end use. Beyond the printing process, these requirements may include varnishing, lacquering, bronzing, and embossing. Other considerations are the labeling application, laminating, compatibility with adhesives, and combination with other materials. The coated side of labels may be white or colored and may be supercalendered, cast-coated, or matte-finished. Labels are used for such applications as box wraps, cigarette packaging, metal can and bottle labels, posters, book jackets, food wraps, pressure-sensitive labels, and lamination to paperboard. When selecting a label paper, printers should give the paper supplier all requirements pertaining to the paper's printing and finishing operations, method of application, and end use. The basic size for label paper is 25×38 in. (635×965 mm), with basis weights of 60 and 70 lb./ream (89 and 104 g/m^2).

LATEX-TREATED PAPERS

These papers have fibers that are impregnated with latex to ensure durability, high-edge tear resistance, wet strength, flexibility, and leather-like properties. They may be stretched, stamped, punched, and embossed in the same manner as leather. Embossed patterns with leather and fabric designs may be applied. Latex-treated papers may be coated for improved printability and resistance to oil, grease, and water. They are used for rugged printed covers, charts, maps, labels, banners, tags, book covers, and children's books.

LEDGER PAPERS

Ledger papers must have good strength, good stiffness, and a hard surface suitable for pen-and-ink writing, erasing, ruling, and data entry. These papers are used for the machine posting of data, which requires a smooth to slightly rough or "postal" finish. Ledger papers are made from all-chemical wood pulp, from a combination of wood and cotton fibers, or from 100% cotton fiber. Typical uses include loose-leaf and bound ledger books, inventory and accounting record systems, wills, deeds, and other long-lasting documents. Ledger papers are made in heavier basis weights than bond papers. They are available in basis weights of 24, 28, 32, and 36 lb./ream (90, 105, 120, and 135 g/m^2), and their basic size is 17×22 in. (432×559 mm).

LIGHTWEIGHT COATED PRINTING PAPER

These grades are usually made from groundwood fibers and have the lowest brightness of the printing-grade family. Lightweight coated groundwood papers are used extensively for high-volume web offset or rotogravure printing of magazines, catalogs, and preprinted newspaper inserts and coupons. Their basic size is 25×38 in. (635×965 mm), and their basic weight ranges from 30 lb. to 40 lb./ream (44 to 59 g/m^2).

Manifold and **onionskin papers** are essentially lightweight bond papers. Manifold papers are available in either machine or unglazed finish, and in a finish machine-glazed on one side for producing distinct carbon copies. Onionskin papers are air-dried and have a cockle, smooth, or calendered finish. Their fiber content may be all-chemical wood, or 25% or 100% cotton fiber. Both types of papers are often ordered grain-short for maximum rigidity in the press-running direction and for better blanket release. Representative uses of manifold and onionskin papers are airmail stationery, lightweight reports, catalogs, manuals, envelope enclosures, advertisements, and carbon copies of legal documents. Regular basis weights, at a basic size of 17×22 in. (432×559 mm), are 8 or 9 lb./ream (30 or 34 g/m^2).

NEWSPRINT

Newsprint is manufactured largely from groundwood pulps and is used primarily for the printing of newspapers. Newsprint traditionally is not surface-sized because it needs to be highly absorbent to allow for the rapid penetration of news ink without the aid of heatset drying. Newsprint used for quality multicolor newspapers, however, is usually sized to give it a stronger and more lint-free surface. Twin-wire paper machines that produce a sheet with less two-sidedness have also improved the quality of newsprint. Most newspapers once printed solely by letterpress are now printed by web offset and flexography. Since newsprint is an inherently weak paper, roll defects can easily precipitate web breaks on high-speed presses. Moisture content must be maintained at a high level, close to 8%, to prevent brittleness and web breaks.

Roto news is made with more finely screened pulp, contains more filler than regular news, and is calendered to the higher finish needed for rotogravure printing. Proper receptivity and holdout for gravure inks, softness and compressibility, freedom from abrasiveness, and rolls free from defects are other essential requirements of roto newspaper. Supercalendered uncoated rotogravure papers containing mechanical pulp and fillers are used as a premium roto paper for the Sunday supplements and magazine sections of newspapers. Newspaper inserts may be printed on newsprint or roto news. However, for more effective printed advertising and reader response, higher quality uncoated and coated papers printed multicolor on heatset presses can be used for newspaper inserts.

PAPERBOARD

The term paperboard refers to paper products that have a higher basis weight, greater thickness—normally at least 12 pt. (0.012 in. or 0.3 mm)—and more rigidity than paper. Some exceptions to this rule are liner board and corrugating medium (whose thickness may be less than 12 pt.) and drawing paper (which may exceed 12 pt. in thickness). The function of paperboard cartons, boxes, and containers is not only to protect the product, but also to advertise and sell it at the point of purchase and to provide instructions for its proper use. Paperboard cartons are used for milk and other beverages. White-lined or coated gray boxboard made from recycled fibers is printed for cereal, soap, and cracker boxes. Strong white-lined unbleached board is printed for applications such as beverage carriers. Solid white (bleached) paperboard of various thicknesses, either coated or uncoated, is printed for folding cartons used to package products like food, cosmetics, candy, and cigarettes.

Solid unbleached sulfate (SUS) paperboard grades are used as a facing material or corrugating medium for corrugated containers, and in the fabrication of cartons and beverage carriers. Solid white bleached paperboard, called solid bleached sulfate or SBS, is widely used for the packaging of food and non-edible products such as plates, dishes, and blister packaging. Recycled paperboard is converted into containers, folding and set-up boxes, cores, and corrugating medium and is used in the manufacture of chipboard.

PARCHMENTS

Artificial parchment, with its mottled appearance, is produced by a special procedure during papermaking. It is available in white and pastel colors and in various weights. Artificial parchment is used for printed products like wine lists, certificates, testimonials, diplomas, announcements, guarantees, and coupons, or anywhere a dignified background for printing is desired.

Vegetable parchment is a unique paper made by passing paper through a sulfuric acid bath that fuses its fibers into a homogenous mass. It has a high wet strength and is greaseproof. Because of its unique appearance and durable hard surface, vegetable parchment is used for etching and drawing applications; wills, deeds, diplomas, and stock certificates; reproductions of historical and religious documents; and other permanent records. Because of its greaseproof surface, vegetable parchment is ideal for certain package enclosures. Special inks are required for printing parchment paper because of this greaseproof surface.

SAFETY PAPERS

Safety papers must be able to expose forgery or document alterations made by either mechanical erasure or chemicals. They also must meet the rigid durability specifications needed in the handling and treatment of bank checks. Safety papers are available with a protective background in various designs and colors. Check paper must have a smooth surface for imprinting sharply defined, unbroken MICR characters (special characters printed on checks with magnetic ink) and for printing pictorial backgrounds. Other critical requirements include adequate bursting and tear strength and the ability to maintain rigidity to withstand repeated handling and many passes through high-speed check-sorting equipment. While the largest use for safety papers is printed checks, they are also used for other negotiable documents that need protection against forgery, such as bonds, deposit slips, coupons, tickets, merchandise certificates, certificates of title, warranties, and legal forms. The standard basis weight, at the basic size of 17×22 in. (432×559 mm), is 24 lb./ream (90 g/m^2).

TAG PAPERS

Tag is made from long-fiber sulfate pulps that have exceptional strength. These papers are calendered to a smooth, hard finish and are available in white, manila, and various other colors. Coated tag papers are used where better printability is required. Typical applications are price tags, file folders, job tickets, jackets, heavy-duty envelopes, and covers. The basic size of tag papers is 24×36 in. (610×914 mm), with basis weights of 100, 125, 150, 175, 200, and 250 lb./ream (163, 203, 244, 285, 325, and 408 g/m^2).

TEXT PAPERS

Text papers are made in many different finishes and textured surfaces, in bright and natural white shades, and in many different colors. Some are watermarked and have deckled edges that lend a degree of elegance and beauty to the paper. Text papers are made in wove, antique, vellum, and felt finishes, which may have light, medium, or heavy pattern-depth embossing. They come in a gamut of colors, including strong bright colors, subdued colors, and pastels. Many grades are available in matching envelopes and cover weights. Text papers offer varied and visually appealing backgrounds for graphic design and are especially suited for programs, announcements, menus, annual reports, and corporate advertising brochures.

UNCOATED MACHINE-FINISH GROUNDWOOD PRINTING PAPERS

These are similar to newsprint but have a smoother surface and higher brightness. They are manufactured with various percentages of fillers to enhance their brightness and printability. Printing applications include catalogs, directories, periodicals, bus transfers, way bills, ballots, and paperbacks.

Supercalendered uncoated groundwood papers are increasingly used for rotogravure printing. These supercalendered papers have a higher percentage of clay filler and more highly refined mechanical pulps than machine-finished groundwood printing papers, providing a superior finish for gravure printing. The print quality of supercalendered uncoated groundwood approaches that of lightweight coated groundwood paper. Printing applications include magazines, catalogs, and the supplement and magazine sections of Sunday newspapers. The basic size of uncoated groundwood printing paper is 25×38 in. (635×965 mm), with basis weights ranging from 20 to 45 lb./ream (30 to 67 g/m^2).

UNCOATED FREE OFFSET PAPERS

These papers are available in both sheetfed and web offset varieties and in many grades, finishes, and colors. Finishes include various smooth, wove, vellum, antique, and embossed patterns. White offset papers range in brightness from 75 to 90 or above, and opaque offset grades offer more opacity and brightness than standard grades. Colored offset lines come in six or more colors. Their uses run the gamut from commercial printing to such applications as personalized computer-generated letters and "business forms" promotional mailings. For book manufacturing, uncoated free sheets can be made to a specified bulk and shade, as well as for specific printing processes and binding requirements. They have a basic size of 25×38 in. (635×965 mm) and basis weights ranging from 45 to 120 lb./ream. (67 to 178 g/m^2).

WEDDING PAPERS

Whether finished as vellum, plate, or linen, wedding papers must have an appearance of quality and the ability to produce sharply engraved characters. Wedding papers are made from chemical wood, cotton fibers, or a combination of cotton and wood fibers. They are made with a very uniform fiber distribution and a nonglare, refined surface. In addition to wedding stationery, wedding papers are used as stationery for executive, professional, and personal use, and for commercial announcements and invitations. Bristol weights are used for business cards, acknowledgments, and announcements. The basic size for wedding papers is 17×22 in. (432×559 mm), with basis weights of 28, 32, 36, and 40 lb./ream (105, 120, 135, and 150 g/m^2).

3 Ordering Paper in Sheets

IMPORTANT SPECIFICATIONS

Size and Ream Weight

When ordering paper in sheets, show the number of sheets, basis weight, size, and total weight on the order. It may be to the buyer's advantage to adjust the total number of sheets upward or downward to take advantage of price breaks.

Number of sheets	100,000
Basis weight	50 lb.
Size	25×38 in.
Total weight	10,000 lb.

When ordering paper in sheets, show the number of sheets, basis weight, size, and total weight on the order. The calculation for total weight is shown on page 7.

If the paper in the above example used "M" weight instead of ream weight, the order would appear as follows:

Number of sheets	100,000
"M" weight	100 lb. (50 × 2)
Size	25×38 in.
Total weight	10,000 lb.

An order listing "M" weight instead of ream weight.

If, in the above example, the sheet size were 34×45 in., the "M" weight would not be 100 lb., but would be 100 lb. times the proportional increase in size of the 35×45-in. sheet over the basic size of 25×38 in.

25 × 38 = 950 sq. in.
35 × 45 = 1,575 sq. in.
1,575 ÷ 950 = 1.68

1.68 × 50 = 84 lb. (ream weight)
84 × 2 = 168 lb. ("M" weight)

Calculating the weight of a non-basic size.

In the above example, the 35×45 specification would be written as 35×45 168M. This specification should then be followed by the basic size and basis weight for that grade category which, for book and label grades, is 25×38—50.

Any time calculations are being made for cost one must be careful not to overlook extra charges such as those for lightweight paper, odd sizes, or quantities that require partial cartons or skids. Above all, always be sure to recheck the figures.

CALIPER AND BULK

If there is a thickness specification for paper in addition to basis weight and finish, it should be stated as an average, minimum, or maximum caliper in thousandths of an inch, or points (micrometers for metric units). Thickness is subject to manufacturing tolerances, as is basis weight. Therefore, if caliper is critical to the job, it should be written with either acceptable plus or minus, no-less-than, or no-more-than tolerances.

COLOR/SHADE

If the grade is made in more than one shade of white or a color, specify the desired shade. To avoid a misunderstanding, submit a sample of the shade or color desired.

GRAIN DIRECTION

State whether the grain is to be long or short, or indicate the dimension for grain direction. For example: if the grain is to run the long dimension of the sheet, it should be written either "25×38 grain-long" or "grain in the 38-in. direction." If grain direction can be either long or short, specify "grain optional." Although the direction of the grain may also be underscored, as in 25×38, it is best not to rely on this method to indicate grain direction. Specifying grain direction is important; otherwise, mills will cut the sheet to fit the parent roll and take the grain as it falls.

TRIMMING

Most sheetfed paper for offset printing must be cut to exact size, and all corners must be square. This is particularly necessary for sheetfed perfecting presses and jobs that are printed "work-and-tumble" or "work-and-flop." Orders for paper printed in this manner should state this requirement. There is a trend toward the precision sheeting of offset printing papers, without the need for guillotine trimming. Precision sheeting produces sheets with edges cleanly cut and without dust and "welding." This is a good system for maintaining sheet squareness and dimensional accuracy.

PRESSROOM CONDITIONS

Specify whether the pressroom is conditioned or unconditioned. If it is conditioned to a constant relative humidity and temperature, state the readings on the order. For a making order, mills may use this information to put the paper's moisture close to pressroom conditions.

SPECIAL REQUIREMENTS

If the paper must meet specific requirements such as special inks (like high-gloss, high-tack, or metallic inks), unusual folding or binding applications, varnishing, lacquering, bronzing, or an out-of-the-ordinary use, the paper supplier should be alerted. If the selected paper is not going to meet these requirements, it is better to know at the outset.

PACKAGING

Always indicate the method of packaging and its pertinent specifications. These specifications include junior or full-size cartons, either unsealed and marked in reams or some fraction thereof, or sealed as a designated number of sheets and skids. Cartons may be palletized for unitized handling and better protection. For proper use by the printer's handling equipment, skid specifications should include weight and height limitations; the number of sheets per skid; the height, direction, and distance between runners; and leg construction, location, and spacing. For uncoated papers, the order should state if there is a preference for packing the paper wire-side or felt-side up.

DELIVERY AND SHIPPING INSTRUCTIONS

The order should state the delivery date required and the days and hours when the paper can be received at its destination. Other required information may include the name of the railroad for a rail siding, platform and unloading restrictions, and whether the destination is a warehouse or the printing plant. Sidewalk or platform delivery should also be noted.

SAMPLE CHECKLIST FOR ORDERING PAPER IN SHEETS

The use of a prepared checklist containing all necessary information will avoid errors and oversights, and give the merchant and paper manufacturer the information required to deliver the proper paper to the printer at the right time and destination. In addition, there should be no discrepancies between the verbal entry of the order and its written confirmation. A checklist increases the probability that the paper ordered will be received on time, in the quantity and quality ordered. Checklists may be obtained from merchants or mills, or customized to fit a particular printer's or user's needs.

The sample checklist shown here has three sections. Section one contains general information such as the name of the person with whom the order was placed, the company's name and address, the

CHECKLIST FOR ORDERING PAPER IN SHEETS

Salesperson ____________________ Date ____________________
Company ____________________ Purchasing agent ____________________
Address ____
Ship-to address ____
Grade ____________________ P.O. # ____________________
Sheet count ____________________ Deliver date ____________________
Basis weight ____________________ Finish ____________________

Grain direction

❑ Long ❑ Short ❑ Either

Paper to be printed

❑ Sheet wise ❑ Work-and-turn ❑ Work-and-tumble

Trimming

❑ Machine ❑ Trim 2 sides ❑ Trim 4 sides

Reproduction method

❑ Letterpress ❑ Gravure ❑ Offset lithography

Packing

❑ Cartons ream-marked
❑ Skids ream-marked
❑ Felt-up
❑ Felt-down

Skid specification

❑ 4-way entry ❑ Short-way runners
❑ 2-way entry ❑ Long-way runners

Maximum weight __________ lb.
Maximum height __________ in.
Maximum distance between runners __________ in.

Skid markings

❑ Mark skid numbers and order number on runners

Shipping

❑ Sidewalk delivery by winch truck
Most satisfactory delivery hours:
________ AM to ________ AM
________ PM to ________ PM
Receiving platform closed from ______ to ______

NOTE: Be sure to send out-turned samples in advance of shipment.

shipping address, paper grade ordered, size and weight, color, date, purchasing agent's name, purchase order number, basis weight, and finish.

Section two contains specific technical information on grain direction and trimming; whether the paper is to be printed sheet wise, work-and-turn, or work-and-tumble; and reproduction method such as letterpress, gravure, silk screen, or offset lithography.

Section three contains information about shipping: whether the paper is to be packed in cartons or on skids, felt side up or down, ream markers or not, and skid specification for handling purposes. It also contains delivery information such as desired delivery hours, location of receiving platform, and any special markings required.

The sample checklist should contain a note in bold type requesting that "out-turned samples be sent in advance of shipment." The purpose for this is to make sure the paper being shipped meets the specifications of the order. This note, along with the rest of the checklist, will help to avoid confusion about what was ordered and the place and time of delivery.

4 Ordering Paper in Rolls

Roll paper is ordered and invoiced on the basis of its gross roll weight, which includes the weight of the wrapping and the weight of a non-returnable core. Rolls having returnable metal cores are normally invoiced for the net weight of the paper, with a separate charge and accounting for the core and a refund of its charge when it is returned to the paper manufacturer. The total area for a roll with a given dimension and weight depends upon the type of paper and its thickness. A paper with the same thickness but higher basis weight will weigh more for the same diameter roll. A thinner paper, wound to a 40-in. (1016-mm) diameter, will have more surface area than a thicker paper wound to that same diameter.

IMPORTANT SPECIFICATIONS

Weight

The basic formula for determining the approximate weight of a roll of paper is as follows:

Roll Diameter Squared × Roll Width × Roll Factor

Antique Finish	0.018
Machine Finish	0.027
Supercalendered Finish	0.030
Coated Two Sides	0.034
Coated One Side	0.030

Roll factors used in determining the approximate weight of a roll of paper.

The following example shows how the formula is put to use in calculating the approximate weight of a roll of machine-finished paper.

Roll Diameter	42 in.
Roll Width	40 in.
Machine Finish	0.027 factor
Calculations:	42 × 42 × 40 × 0.027 = 1905.12 lb.

Calculating the weight of a roll of machine-finish paper.

Linear Footage

The basic formula for determining linear footage is as follows:

$$\frac{\text{Weight of Roll (in pounds)} \times \text{Basic Size} \times 500}{\text{Width of Roll (in inches)} \times 12 \text{ in.} \times \text{Basis Weight}}$$

Weight of Roll = 2000 lb.
Basic Size = 25×38 in.
Basis Weight = 55 lb.
Width of Roll = 40 in.

$$\frac{2000 \times 25 \times 38 \times 500}{40 \times 12 \times 55} = 35{,}985 \text{ linear feet}$$

Calculating the linear footage of a roll of paper.

It must be remembered that the actual basis weight may not be exactly as indicated. In the above example basis weight is assumed to be exactly 55 lb. However, the basis weight can vary, so the actual paper in the roll may be slightly more or less than this. The linear footage will be more (giving more printed copies) if the basis weight is below 55 lb. It will be less (giving fewer printed copies) if the basis weight is above 55 lb. The industry considers a variation in basis weight of ±5% as the norm, and any order that is within this variation is considered a good delivery. Each mill, however, has its own specification requirements. When ordering paper it is always prudent to check with the mill supplying the paper. This is important information when determining the waste for a given job. If the paper ordered had a basis weight 5% heavier than the stated basis weight there would be an automatic paper loss of 5%. For this reason, it is best to order rolls of paper by the linear foot and not by weight. Some manufacturers indicate the total footage or length of paper on each roll. Check with your supplier to see if that option is available.

Orders for rolls of paper must also make allowance for waste, which includes the wrapping and roll stripping, core and core waste (which can amount to 3% or more), and on-press and binding waste.

The amount of paper ordered is also a factor in the percentage of over- or underruns. For example, an order of book paper for less than 5000 lb. will have a ±20% variation, while 40,000 lb. or more will ship with an over or under variation of only 3%. Again it is wise to check with the paper manufacturer or paper merchant to find out their accepted variation.

Roll Dimensions

Roll width and diameter should be individually stated. Since paper manufacturers have a plus-or-minus width tolerance, printing requirements that cannot have rolls exceed or be less than a specified width should be clearly indicated so that the manufacturer's tolerances can be properly fitted to the specific requirement.

Maximum Diameter

It is usually desirable to maximize roll diameter in order to minimize the number of roll changes on the press. Manufacturing tolerances for diameter are normally ±1 in. (±25.4 mm) from the ordered diameter. Caution should be taken when ordering maximum diameter, to ensure that this maximum diameter plus the manufacturer's tolerance does not exceed the capacity of the infeed reel stand weight and space. Mills may have additional charges for narrow-width rolls and rolls of small diameter.

Basis Weight and Thickness

A manufacturing basis weight tolerance generally applies to rolls, as it does to sheets. When ordering basis weights higher than normal for web printing, precautions should be taken that the paper's thickness does not create problems with on-press folding and handling or cause blistering in the hot-air dryers.

Side Out

If the printer prefers that either the wire or felt side of the paper be wound on the outside of the roll, it should be indicated on the order.

Splicing

Heatset printing generally requires the use of heat-resistant splicing tape. Therefore, a heat-resistant splicing tape should be specified on the order. Splices may be made straight across or diagonally across the web. Diagonal splices have less tendency to catch on parts of the press. Splice locations can be indicated by the mill with flags or markings on each end of the roll.

Core Specifications

Always specify core type—returnable or non-returnable—and core dimensions. Include such details as inside diameter, ends with or without slots, and dimensions of the slotted ends for the printer's keyways.

Printing Requirements

The process by which the paper will be printed is vital information. Printers should indicate whether the paper will be printed on heatset or non-heatset web presses. For coated paper, heatset requirements should be clearly specified and should include the manufacturer, model name, and length of the heatset drying equipment. If heatset drying equipment is to be used (like flame-impingement dryers that place extra demands on paper for blister resistance), this fact should be known to the paper supplier, along with the amount of ink coverage and the paper's exit temperature from the dryer.

CHECKLIST FOR ORDERING PAPER IN ROLLS

Salesperson ______________________ Date ____________________
Company ________________________ Purchasing agent____________
Address ____
Shipping address ____
P.O. # __________________________ Delivery date ______________

Grade __________________________________
Quantity ______________________________ lb.
Maximum roll width _____________________ in.
Maximum roll diameter ___________________ in.
Core Inside diameter _____________________ in.
Type of press _____________________________
Speed of press ____________________________
Maximum ink-drying temperature _____________

Type of Core

❑ Returnable ❑ Non-returnable
❑ Slotted ❑ Non-slotted ❑ Slots in juxtaposition

Roll Winding

❑ Felt side OUT ❑ Felt side IN

Note: Mark directional arrows on wrapper

Splicing (maximum acceptable to roll): ________________

Flag:

❑ One side ❑ Two sides ❑ Diagonally
❑ Use 3M splicing material for heatset reproduction

Delivery

❑ On side ❑ On end

Special Instructions

____
____
____
____
____
____

Since the types of paper and specifications required for web offset and sheetfed offset printing are generally different, printers should distinguish between rolls for web printing and rolls for inplant or in-line press sheeting.

Roll Packaging

All pertinent information for roll identity and use should appear on the packaging. This information should include grade name, order numbers, roll dimensions, weight, mill roll number, number of splices, and direction of unwind. For easy identification in warehouse storage, these specifications may appear in two different locations on the roll wrapping. It may also help to indicate certain identifying information on the end of an unwrapped roll near its core.

Delivery and Shipping Instructions

If rolls should be shipped on their ends or sides for a specific reason, this should be stated on the order. Any special instructions or restrictions that apply to receiving, unloading, roll handling, and equipment capacity also should be noted, along with the delivery date required and the days and hours when paper can be received. For rail shipment, the name of the railroad servicing the printer's rail siding should be indicated.

5 How Paper is Priced

As with most products, paper prices respond to supply and demand. Prices increase for a variety of reasons, the most common one being that demand exceeds mill production capacity. Prices also increase when paper manufacturers try to recover costs associated with an increase in the price of material, energy, or shipping. The paper industry is highly competitive—prices will decrease as paper mills expand their papermaking capacity and increase when that capacity approaches its limits. It is always advisable to compare prices between merchants and mills and be aware when new paper machines start up. Many times a mill will sell its start-up tonnage at a lower price.

The industry uses brackets or segments for establishing prices. Cut-size and full-size sheets are two such segments. Cut-sizes papers are usually less than 11×17 in. with the majority being 8½×11 in. These papers are mostly used for copiers and computer printers. They are priced by the sheet and sold by the ream or carton. Full-size sheets are, as the term suggests, standard sheets for the grade and are sold in cartons, skids, or carload lots, and they are priced by the hundredweight (cwt).

Both cut-size and full-size sheets have price brackets based on the amount of paper purchased. The amount of paper represented by each bracket may vary between grades; therefore, it is prudent to check with the merchant or mill to be sure of the number of sheets in each bracket. The following chart shows typical price brackets. In this example, if you purchased 3–9 cartons of cut-size paper, the price per carton would be slightly less than if you purchased 1–2 cartons of cut-size paper.

	Number of cartons					Pounds
Cut-size	<1	1	3	10	40	
Full-size	<1	1	4	16	24	5000 lb.

Typical merchant price brackets, per carton or pounds.

Price brackets are common for all merchant and mill sales, however the price for each bracket can and does vary between suppliers. It is always prudent to compare prices between suppliers and within the price brackets. When ordering paper it is important to be aware and understand these price brackets. For example, if an order calls for less than a carton it may be more economical to order a full carton—to "round" orders up—because of the price break at the one-carton level. If a job requires 4,850 sheets, it may actually be cheaper to order five cartons (5,000 sheets).

Additional costs are usually incurred any time special handling is required. If an order calls for a size that is not standard, there will usually be a 10% up-charge. This means that a size that is not a standard size or not commonly stocked will usually cost more than a larger standard size. An order requiring 2000 sheets of a non-standard 36×48-in. paper may cost more than 2000 sheets of standard 38×50 in. It is always wise to check with the paper supplier when an order requires special considerations like unusual sizes or quantities, especially if it is close to a price bracket or a standard size.

6 How to Place a Making Order

Standard paper sizes and weights are those most commonly used, and they are generally stocked by paper mills and merchants. However, almost any size and weight of paper can be purchased. Sizes and weights other than standard are usually ordered through paper merchants or direct from the mills. Ordering paper that is not stocked is referred to as a ***making order.*** When a purchaser has a set of sheet specifications that doesn't fit standard sizes or weight, a making order may be required.

If a making order is not large enough to justify changing over the paper machine, the non-standard size will be cut from a larger sheet. This makes for a more expensive order due to waste and additional labor. Making orders that are large enough to change over the paper machine are usually from large publishers who use tons of paper on a regular basis.

It is always more economical to design pieces that fit standard-sized papers. However, if a job requires a size other than standard, it may be cheaper to order the next size up instead of placing a making order. If, for example, the required size is between 36×48 in. and 38×50 in., it will normally be less expensive to order the 38×50-in. size. Always compare the cost of a special size against the cost of a standard size before placing the order.

Placing a making order requires a clear set of specifications. For example, it is important to specify the grain direction if the job calls for the grain to run in a particular direction. If the order doesn't specify grain direction, mills will process the order with the grain running in the direction that gives the highest yield.

Making orders are subject to a permissible plus-or-minus percentage variation in the delivered quantity. When a making order states "not more than" or "not less than" the ordered quantity, the permissible one-way variation in delivered quantity is double that which applies to a plus-or-minus variation. For example, if the permissible variation is ±5% on a making order, the one-way variation becomes 10% if the order reads "not more than" or "not less than" the ordered quantity. Because each paper mill ships to a different percent variation, paper users should thoroughly understand this aspect of making orders and ask the paper supplier to provide the percent variation applicable to their specific orders.

A making order allows greater choice in weight, size, finish, color, and caliper. It is appropriate to stress again the importance of having a clear and complete set of specifications accompany a making order. This is because the purchaser owns the paper. If it is not suitable for the job, it is difficult to resell, whereas an order of standard paper that doesn't meet end-use requirements can be exchanged by the mill or merchant for paper that does meet these requirements. It is, therefore, prudent to use a checklist when placing a making order.

7 Paper Spoilage Allowance

The most common sources of spoilage include damage from shipping and handling, trim, press makeready, and bindery makeready. Waste or spoilage from trim and makeready can be predetermined. More difficult to estimate is damage which occurs during shipping and handling. Rolls may be dropped on their edges, run into by tow motors, or rolled across a floor that is littered with debris. Paper in skids or cartons may be damaged by tow motors, water dripping from the ceiling, or improper rewrapping or storage.

Estimating the paper spoilage allowance requires the buyer to know the history of shipping and handling damage in order to make an educated guess. Fortunately, there are guides for predicting spoilage due to bindery and printing needs.

Number of sheets printed	1 color/ 1 side	Each additional color	1 color/ 2 sides	Each additional color
250	25%	20%	35%	30%
500	12%	10%	15%	13%
1,000	10%	8%	11%	9%
2,500	8%	6%	10%	8%
5,000	5%	4%	7%	6%
10,000	4%	3%	6%	5%
25,000	3%	2%	5%	4%

Guide for printing and bindery spoilage (from The Paper Buyers' Encyclopedia*).*

For example, assume that 5,000 sheets of paper are printed with three colors on both sides. Referring to the chart on the previous page, find the spoilage associated with printing "1 color/2 sides" for 5,000 sheets, which in this case is 7%. Next find the spoilage for each additional color for 5,000 sheets, which is 6%. This number (6%) must be doubled because there are two additional colors. In this example, the paper spoilage allowance is 19%:

7% (1 color/2 sides) + 12% (2 add'l colors at 6% each)= 19%

The extra paper needed for spoilage is determined by multiplying the number of sheets by the percent calculated for spoilage. In the above example, this equals 950 sheets for spoilage:

0.19 (19%) × 5,000 sheets = 950 extra sheets

The percent of spoilage varies with the number of sheets because the amount needed for printing and bindery is the same no matter how many sheets are printed or bound. Therefore, with the number of sheets required for spoilage remaining the same, the percent for spoilage will be smaller as the number of sheets printed increases. There is one caution, however: if the number of sheets is large enough to require blanket washes during the printing operation, mechanical adjustments, or other equipment-related problems for the press or bindery operations, then additional sheets should be included.

8 Sampling Programs

Buying and ordering the proper paper is made easier with a good paper sampling program. A properly maintained, reliable, and readily accessible sampling of papers can be an essential tool for printers. A sampling program should begin with current quality samples identified by their date of receipt. File samples should be systematically updated according to a schedule arranged with paper suppliers. Suppliers should agree to automatically update the samples when a change occurs in color, shade, or quality, or when items of a sampled grade are added or deleted.

To be practical and useful, filing systems should protect samples from dust, dirt, and exposure to the atmosphere, and they should facilitate sample replacement and retrieval. Sampling the many types and grades of paper used for printing is no easy task, but it should not be left to chance. It requires a constant review and update of various sample books and files to make certain they represent the *current* quality, shade, and color for each grade. Samples of current quality are particularly relevant for jobs that must meet critical paper specifications. Rather than attempting to sample many different types of papers and keep them updated, experienced buyers may elect to sample only those papers used most frequently and to request samples of paper used less frequently on an as-needed basis. The usefulness of a sampling program may justify appointing someone to keep it updated. It may seem like a lot of bother to keep samples current. However, it is more bothersome and more costly to order paper and find out, upon delivery, that it is wrong for the job.

PROPER PROCEDURES FOR VISUAL COMPARISON

When two or more paper samples are compared for shade, color, or brightness, each sample should be backed up by several other samples of itself. This procedure eliminates possible errors in visual judgment resulting from the influence of show-through caused by low opacity of a single-sheet thickness of a sample. During a visual comparison for shade, brightness, or color, the position of samples should be interchanged to avoid a possible bias caused by having viewed them in one relationship only. In visual paper comparisons, the influence of finish patterns (such as laid finish) and grain direction on surface finish, gloss, and brightness should not be overlooked. For uncoated papers, differences between the wire and felt sides can influence the way in which they are visually assessed. Consequently, samples of different papers should be compared when their grain is running in the same direction and, with uncoated papers, when their same side—felt or wire—faces the observer.

Illumination has a pronounced influence upon the visual comparison of white and colored papers. Papers should be viewed in northern daylight or the artificially simulated daylight of color-matching booths. The 6500 K level of illumination, described in TAPPI (Technical Association of the Pulp and Paper Industry) Official Test Method T 515, is the preferred level for visual comparison of white and colored papers. White papers containing optical or fluorescent brighteners will appear to have different brightness levels when viewed under daylight, indoor incandescent, and indoor fluorescent illumination. For this reason, it may be advisable to examine these papers under the different available lighting conditions, including fluorescent lamp light.

USING SAMPLES IN PAPER SELECTION

Paper choices should be made at the beginning of the production cycle and based on production end-use and design requirements as well as customer expectations. It is not unusual for paper to be specified by someone who may not know its end-use requirements

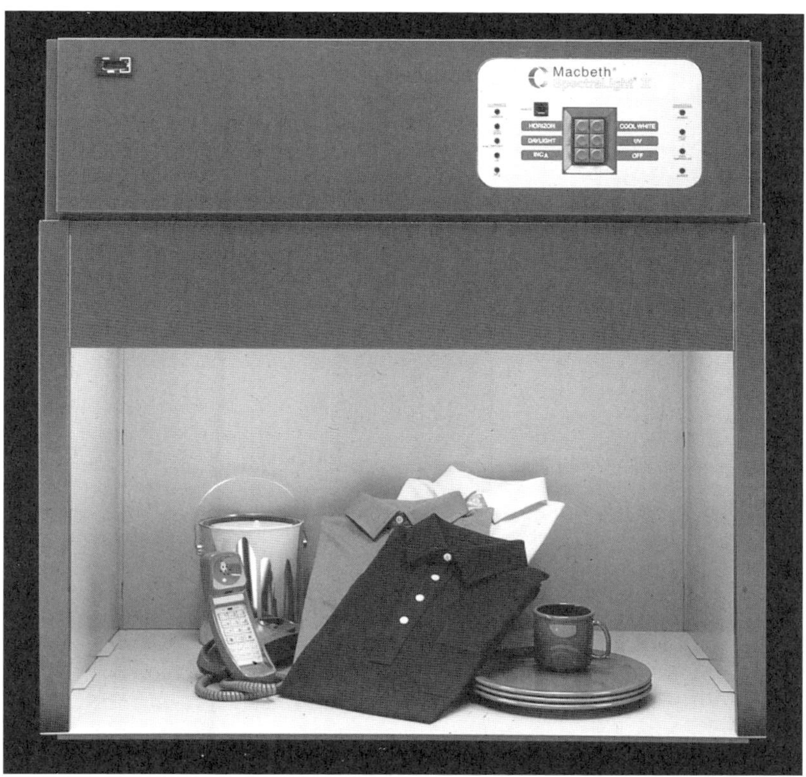

A viewing booth that simulates outdoor light is recommended when making color comparisons. However, other light sources such as incandescent and fluorescent lights should also be used to determine the effect of different lighting on paper appearance. The booth shown above (Spectralight II®) provides four common light-sky conditions (horizon, daylight, incandescent, and cool white) and ultraviolet. (Courtesy GretagMacbeth)

or the capabilities of a particular printing process. This lack of understanding may lead to increased waste, higher cost, failure to meet customer needs, and missed deadlines. It is, therefore, important that all interested parties—the customer, production manager, designer, and paper buyer—provide input before paper is ordered.

One example of a paper property that must be agreed on, if the paper is a "white" printing paper, is its whiteness. There are multiple shades of white paper available, enough to cause miscommuni-

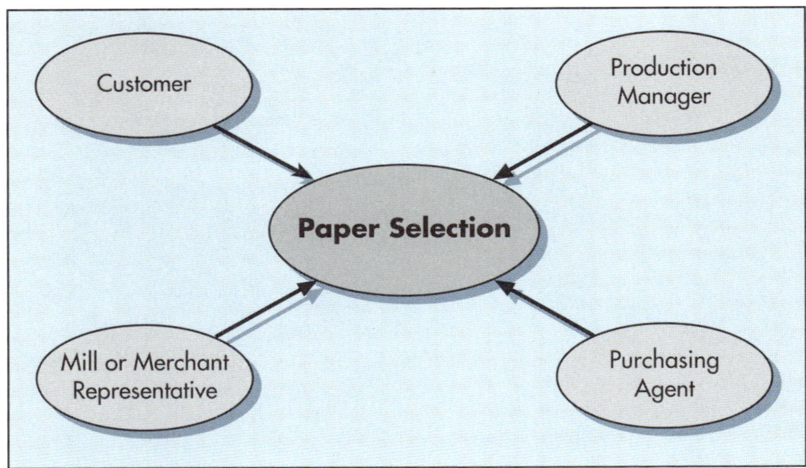

The choice of paper should be made at the beginning of the production cycle with input from the customer, production manager, mill or merchant representative, and purchasing agent.

cation between art director, publisher, customer, and printer. Is it warm white, cream white, cool white, or bright white? One mill's cream white is not the same shade as another mill's cream white. To help bridge this communication gap, a sample of the selected paper should be requested from the mill or paper merchant before the order is placed. Everyone, including the designer and customer, should view the sample under standard lighting conditions and "sign off" on the selection. A sample of the selected paper should accompany the job folder throughout the printing process.

Colored paper also varies from mill to mill, and a conscious effort should be made to clearly identify the chosen color. Again, a paper sample should be obtained, viewed by the appropriate people, and attached to the job ticket. Another identical sample should be kept on file. Obtaining and using samples to identify the paper ahead of time is an insurance policy against frustration, disappointment, and extra work.

Other properties that influence the selection of paper are finish and surface texture. These properties vary—as do color, shade, and

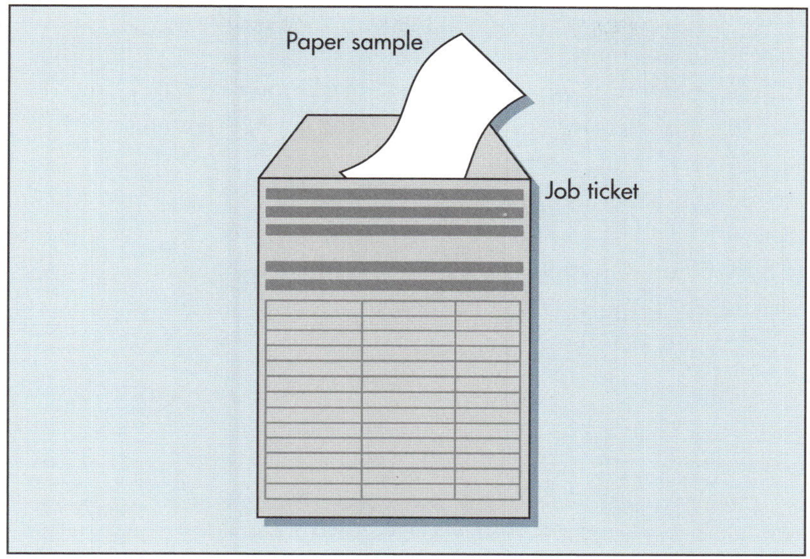

A sample should be attached to the job ticket, with another sample kept on file.

brightness—from mill to mill, underscoring the need for an actual paper sample that represents the paper ordered.

Paper must also meet numerous printing process requirements. It must meet the physical and environmental demands of folding, binding, and converting operations. Choosing the wrong paper for the job can cost money, time, and sleep. Aesthetic and technical requirements mandate that knowledgeable papermakers, designers, and printers assist each other in selecting the right paper for the job.

Knowledge of the kinds of paper available and the proper procedures for specifying and ordering paper is necessary in selecting the right paper. For example, paper merchants carry equivalent papers from various mills, and it is not uncommon for them to suggest that one mill's paper be substituted for another's. The person placing the order should be aware that paper characteristics may vary from mill to mill, and be prepared to make choices based on a knowledge of these differences. Otherwise the "equivalent" paper may not meet end-use requirements or customer expectations. This is another reason for obtaining paper samples prior to ordering the paper. Mills or merchants will supply a sample that represents the shipment before shipping the order. The printer or buyer should always compare this sample, as well as the actual shipment, to the sample used in the decision-making process.

In addition to securing unprinted samples from merchants or mills it is prudent to also ask for *printed* samples of the paper under consideration. Most mills and merchants maintain a library of samples for this purpose. These printed samples will give an indication of ink gloss, ink density, printing contrast, and in many cases foldability.

9 Paper Conditioning

Buying paper requires not only an understanding of how to acquire the right paper at the best price, but also an understanding of how to protect the paper that has been ordered and delivered. Improper storing and handling of paper will create waste and paper shortages, increasing cost, delays, and unhappy customers.

Moisture is one element that must be considered when storing and preparing paper for press or bindery operations. The ability of paper fibers to gain or lose moisture easily can result in runnability and register problems, and has a great impact on sheetfed papers. Printers therefore should know how moisture behaves and how to measure and control it. Moisture is always present in the atmosphere and is usually referred to as water vapor or humidity. **Absolute humidity** is the total weight of water contained in a given volume of air, expressed as pounds of water per pound of dry air. The atmosphere is said to be saturated when its air contains the maximum amount of water it can hold.

When saturated air is cooled, its capacity to hold water vapor is decreased, forcing some of the water to condense or change back into a liquid. Likewise, when air temperature is raised, its capacity to hold moisture is increased. The temperature at which air becomes saturated is referred to as its **dew point.** The ratio of the quantity of vapor present in the air to the maximum amount the air could hold at a given temperature is called its **relative humidity** (RH). When the relative humidity is 50%, the air contains only 50% of the moisture it could contain at that specific temperature.

Temperature		Relative Humidity
100°F	38°C	24%
95	35	28
90	32	32
85	29	38
80	27	45
75	24	52
70	21	62
65	18	74
60	16	88
56	13	100

Example: A pressroom environment is maintained at 45% RH and 80°F (27°C). At the end of the day, the air conditioning and heat are turned off and the room is closed. The next morning the pressroom temperature is 65°F (18°C). The total amount of moisture vapor in the air remains the same, but the relative humidity has risen to 74%. This increase in relative humidity would have caused any exposed paper to develop wavy edges.

Effect that a change in temperature has on relative humidity when absolute humidity remains constant.

Paper reaches what is referred to as **equilibrium relative humidity** when its moisture is in balance with the relative humidity of the air. When paper reaches equilibrium relative humidity, it will neither gain nor lose moisture. To accurately measure the equilibrium relative humidity of paper at a specified temperature, the printer should precisely perform the following test, measuring the relative humidity and temperature immediately surrounding sheets of paper while excluding the influence of the external atmosphere. For skids or stacks of paper, insert a probe or sword-shaped blade between sheets so that its humidity- and temperature-sensing elements are isolated from the external atmosphere and will measure just the atmosphere surrounding the paper. To measure relative humidity and temperature of roll paper, cut through four or five layers of paper with a sharp blade extending 7–10 in. (178–254 mm) inward from one roll edge. Lay the probe flat against the exposed paper and quickly cover it by taping the outer layers back into place.

Humidity, or water vapor, in the air can be measured with such instruments as hygrometers or sling psychrometers. Mechanical hygrometers use hair, nylon, paper, or membranes whose dimensions change when exposed to different humidities. Because mechanical hygrometers are dependent on these types of materials, they are not very sensitive or accurate. A sling psychrometer uses wet- and dry-bulb thermometers, and tables, to measure relative humidity. A properly used sling psychrometer gives accurate readings. Without careful maintenance and the use of proper procedures, however, wet- and dry-bulb psychrometers can give misleading results.

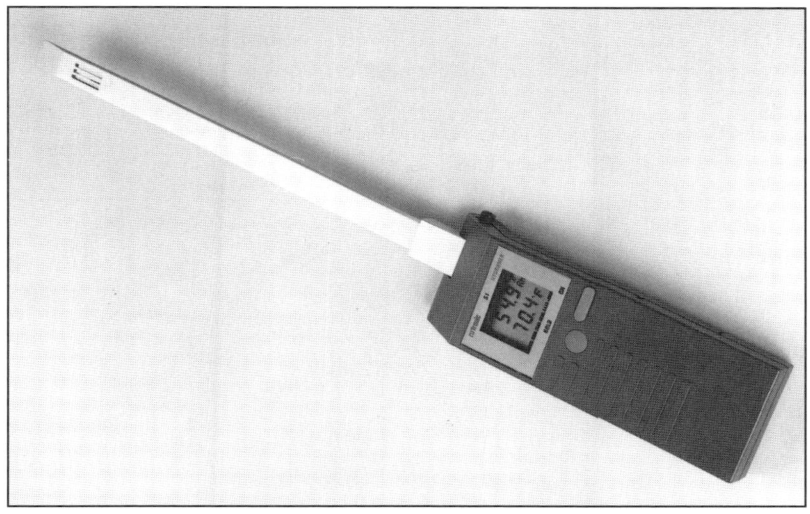

The Rotronic PS1 sword probe, which measures temperature and relative humidity when inserted into a stack or roll of paper. (Courtesy Rotronic Instrument Corp.)

Electronic hygrometers, because of their high sensitivity, accuracy, and dependability, are highly desirable for pressrooms. An accurate electronic hygrometer is especially useful in recording atmospheric changes and performance of air-conditioning equipment. Its dependable data can also be used to diagnose moisture-related paper problems.

Because paper has its best dimensional stability in the range of 35–50% RH, good sheetfed printing is best accomplished with a pressroom temperature of 70–85°F (21–29°C) and an RH of 35–50%. An RH in the 40–45% range has been found to be optimum for many sheetfed offset plants. Paper that is in equilibrium with the atmosphere will usually remain stable throughout the printing operation.

Paper not in balance with the surrounding atmosphere should be kept in a moisture-barrier wrapper at all times. Pressrooms that are kept at an RH of 40–50% and a temperature of 70–85°F are more conducive to inks that dry by oxidation and polymerization because such inks dry faster at higher temperatures and a lower RH. Cold paper brought into a warm pressroom cools the surrounding air and changes the relative humidity of that air. For example, a paper at 56°F (13°C) brought into a pressroom, with a temperature of 75°F (24°C), changes the relative humidity of the surrounding air from 52% to 100%. This change in relative humidity causes the surrounding air to become saturated, resulting in condensation. If the paper is unwrapped and unprotected it will become damp and the condensation will cause wavy edges that cannot be removed completely by ordinary paper conditioning methods. Keeping the cold paper wrapped until it reaches the pressroom temperature will prevent condensation.

A reverse situation occurs when warmer paper is brought into a cooler pressroom. The higher paper temperature warms the surrounding air and lowers its relative humidity. Instead of moisture condensing on the edges and surface of the paper, moisture moves from the paper into the surrounding air. This loss of moisture causes the paper to shrink, which, in turn, creates tight edges.

Paper with a temperature that is warmer or cooler than the pressroom should be given time to reach pressroom temperature. The length of time required to temperature-condition paper depends on the difference between paper and pressroom temperature and the size or volume of the skid, roll, or carton. The following charts indicate the time required for various volumes and

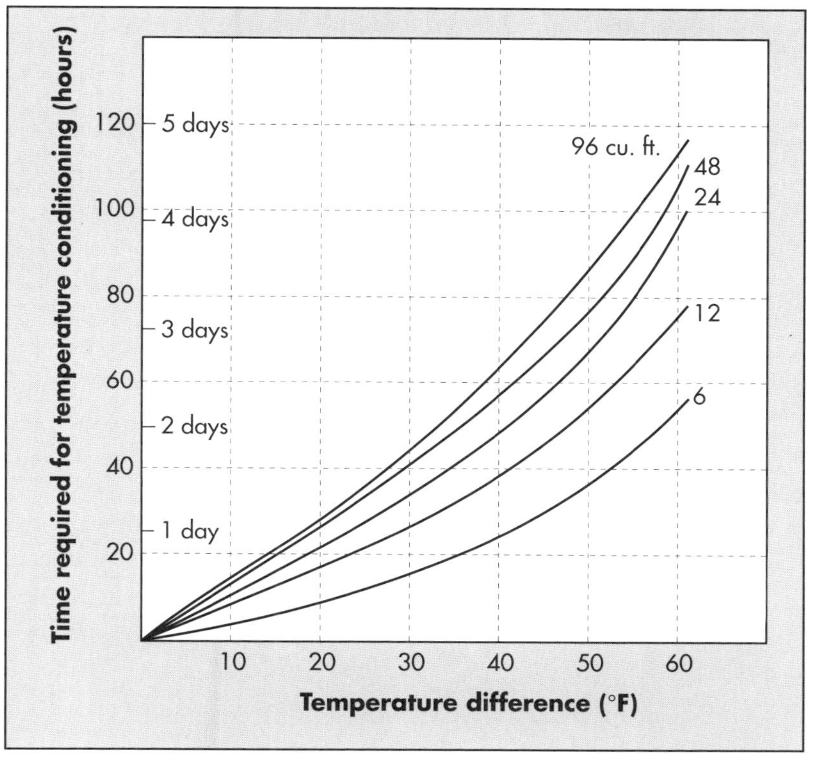

A temperature conditioning chart for paper, expressed in American units.

temperature differentials between paper and pressroom. The time required for paper to become conditioned to pressroom temperature can be read from the chart when the following information is known: the difference in paper and pressroom temperature and the volume of the paper. To find the approximate temperature of paper on skids or in cartons, make a small hole in the wrapper and insert a steel-jacketed thermometer into the pile. Read the temperature after it becomes constant, remove the thermometer, and seal the hole with tape. For rolls, place the thermometer between the wrapper and roll end, since it is not possible to insert it between roll layers without damaging the paper. The volume of skids, car-

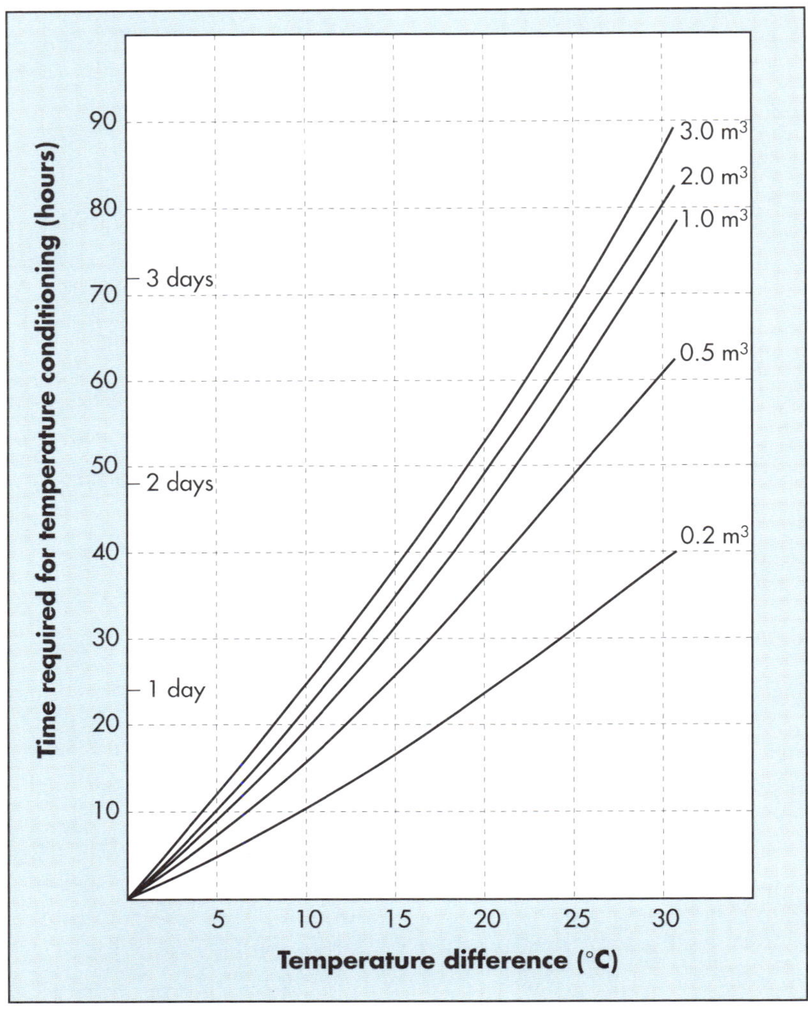

A temperature conditioning chart for paper, expressed in metric units.

tons, and rolls of paper can be determined using the equations on the facing page.

The first step in finding the required time for temperature conditioning is to determine the volume of paper on the skid. Example: A 48-in.-high (1,220-mm) skid of 25×38-in. (635×965-mm) paper is at 45°F (7°C), and the pressroom temperature is 75°F (24°C).

Skid or Carton Volume

$$\text{Volume (ft.}^3) = \frac{\text{Length} \times \text{Width} \times \text{Height (in inches)}}{1{,}728}$$

$$\text{Volume (m}^3) = \frac{\text{Length} \times \text{Width} \times \text{Height (in centimeters)}}{1{,}000{,}000}$$

Equation to determine the volume of paper in a skid or carton.

Roll Volume

$$\text{Volume (ft.}^3) = \frac{\text{Diameter} \times \text{Diameter} \times \text{Length (in inches)}}{2{,}200}$$

$$\text{Volume (m}^3) = \frac{\text{Diameter} \times \text{Diameter} \times \text{Length (in centimeters)}}{1{,}273{,}326}$$

Equation to determine the volume of paper in a roll.

$$\text{Cubic Feet} = \frac{25 \text{ in.} \times 38 \text{ in.} \times 48 \text{ in.}}{1{,}728} = 26 \text{ ft.}^3$$

$$\text{Cubic Meters} = \frac{63.5 \text{ cm} \times 96.5 \text{ cm} \times 121.9 \text{ cm}}{1{,}000{,}000} = 0.75 \text{ m}^3$$

The next step is to determine the temperature difference between the paper and the pressroom. In the above example that difference is 75°F (pressroom) minus 45°F (paper temperature) which equals 30°F (24°C – 7°C = 17°).

To find the required time for temperature-conditioning, locate 30°F (difference between pressroom and paper) on the baseline of the chart for American units (17°C on the chart for metric units) and follow the vertical line to the curve for the volume closest to 26 ft.^{3} (0.75 m^3), and follow the horizontal line to the time axis on the left. Here, the minimum time for temperature-conditioning before unwrapping the skid is 35 hr.

Printers unable to store paper in a heated warehouse should set aside space in the pressroom for temperature-conditioning. Paper should be ordered far enough in advance to allow it to be temperature-conditioned.

To minimize edge distortion and problems in the bindery due to changes in moisture, printed loads should be rewrapped immediately after each pass through the press and after printing. Sometimes it is necessary to run smaller loads and rewrap them immediately after printing. Between printings, reusable plastic moisture-proof covers that fit tightly around printed loads can provide convenient and excellent protection against dimensional change and edge distortion. Paper should not be cut any further in advance of going to press than necessary and should be protected with moisture-proof wrapping immediately after cutting. Skids opened for makeready paper, as well as leftover paper, should be promptly rewrapped before being returned to storage.

10 Handling Paper Complaints

Printers are responsible for getting the job out on time, meeting customer needs, and recovering any losses associated with problems caused by paper or other input materials. Paper merchants and papermakers are responsible for meeting the needs of printers and their customers and, if necessary, replacing any defective material and providing compensation for losses that are directly related to paper.

Although the printer and papermaker's responsibilities are very similar, the emergence of a complaint can initially put more pressure on the printer. Most paper manufacturers will replace a particular paper or compensate for lost time and wasted material if they have evidence showing that the paper is defective or is the most probable cause of a problem at the printing plant. Evidence for paper problems comes primarily from paper mill records and the pressroom. Mill records will usually show that the paper met specified standards when it was shipped because manufacturer's policy is to recycle or send paper to the seconds market if it doesn't meet set standards. The evidence that a paper is defective is usually found in the pressroom, so it therefore becomes the responsibility of the printer to provide the necessary proof that paper was the cause of a particular problem.

Customers usually handle paper problems either by switching manufacturers or by mentioning the problem to the suppliers and absorbing the loss. Other customers will report a problem with no supporting evidence, and expect the supplier to automatically pay for all losses. While these approaches to paper problems offer some degree of satisfaction, they do not provide insight into solving present and future paper problems, nor do they support fair and equitable settlements. For this reason, the customer should have a solid complaint handling system in place to manage paper problems. As part of this system, the problem should be immediately reported to the paper merchant or mill, and supporting evidence and data should be gathered, recorded, and submitted. The printer is essentially the only one in a position to collect the real-time data and samples necessary to support a complaint. The customer's place of business is the "scene of the crime," where clues and evidence exist for supporting a claim.

The first action a customer should take when a paper problem arises is to notify the merchant or mill representative. This early warning of a potential problem gives the paper supplier an opportunity to provide input before waste and lost production time is incurred. If a decision must be made to continue the job with the paper that is causing a problem, it should be made in cooperation with the paper supplier. Continuing to use problem paper without informing the paper supplier or allowing for input may lead to disagreements that frustrate later attempts at a financial settlement. To be able to recommend other paper as a possible cure for a paper problem, paper manufacturers need information that will pinpoint specifically when the paper was made, the paper machine on which it was made, and its exact location across the paper machine reel. Knowing this, papermakers can advise the printer to try paper from another part of the order or even from an entirely different order. It is not unusual for a change in paper to solve the problem. Acquiring information about paper that runs trouble-free can be as important to the paper manufacturer as getting information about problem paper.

COMPLAINT HANDLING PROCESS

It is in the printer's best interest to have a complaint handling process that makes it easy to collect appropriate samples, data, and information needed to support a claim. Following is a brief outline

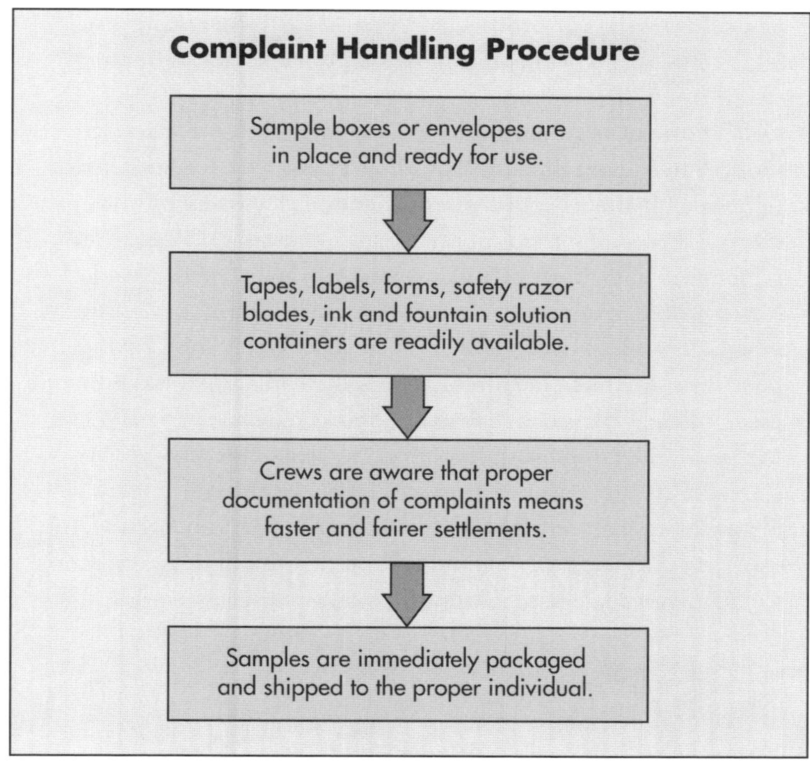

Having a good complaint handling system in place improves the chances for a fair settlement.

of a complaint handling system, including some general procedures that should be followed in collecting evidence at the time of printing.

- Establish a process to report complaints, collect samples, and assemble evidence of paper problems.
- Educate everyone involved in production on the importance of collecting vital information and train him or her to use the proper collecting procedures.
- For a problem involving press sheets, collect and staple together twelve consecutive sheets from the feeder; for roll problems, strip three to four wraps from the roll where the problem occurred. Immediately label the samples.

- Collect twelve consecutive sheets or signatures (showing the problem) from the delivery and immediately staple and label these samples.
- Collect ink and fountain solution samples from the trays and immediately label the containers. Use plastic bottles with watertight lids for the fountain solution and plastic or metal cans with lids for the ink. Don't use paper cups for samples! Paper cup containers will absorb water and solvents and may tear and leak.
- If the problem stems from blanket contamination, pull samples of the debris from the blanket using tape. Don't fold the tape back onto itself or attach it to paper. Instead, attach the tape to a piece of clear plastic. Because the debris may be carried in with the paper, it is important to collect twelve consecutive sheets from the feeder. Again, staple and label the sheets.
- Set aside any unused problem paper, cover the paper with a moisture-barrier material, and label it as complaint paper, with job name and paper mill identification numbers.

COMPLAINT SAMPLING SYSTEM

Most paper mills have extensive testing capabilities to generate data for solving paper- and print-related problems. In addition to paper-testing technology, they have the ability to test inks, fountain solution, and blankets. Since mills generally perform tests in response to a printer's complaint, they will routinely ask for samples of the paper, ink, and fountain solution that was on the press at the time of the problem, along with other pertinent information.

The customer should establish a detailed process for collecting and saving the evidence and data accrued while the problem was occurring. The way to do this is to set up a sampling system that efficiently collects all identifying information from the labels, tickets, and cards associated with each carton, skid, and roll, along with samples of ink and fountain solution. The basis of a sampling system is an easily accessible depository for material, placed at the point where information and samples are collected. This depository may take the form of large individual envelopes or boxes with distinct markings that identify the containers as complaint material. These boxes or envelopes should contain small metal or plastic containers, with lids, for collecting ink and fountain solution. Markers, for labeling, tape for collecting debris from blankets, and razor blades for cutting paper and scraping blankets should also be included in the complaint boxes or envelopes.

All paper, ink, and fountain solution samples, along with written remarks and records associated with the job, should be placed in these containers and kept until the complaint is settled. Since it is in the merchant's interest to identify paper problems, most papermakers are glad to provide help in setting up a complaint system, and they may even supply the material needed to collect and save samples.

Sampling

To be helpful to the papermaker, samples of paper problems must be obtained in the proper amounts and must be properly arranged and labeled. Following is the proper sampling procedure for a picking problem that occurs due to differences in sheeted roll paper.

Multiple webs of paper, usually from three to five rolls, are cut together for filling skid and carton orders. It is possible that each roll within this set has different properties like smoothness, gloss, strength, or absorption. This variation in rolls used to generate sheeted paper will be reflected in the skids or cartons. Since the picking problem may be caused by paper from only one of the rolls, it is important to sample at least twelve consecutive sheets to be sure the offending sheet is included at least twice in the sample. Twelve sheets that include the offending sheet at least twice from both the feeder and delivery can show a pattern pointing to paper as the probable cause of the problem.

In assembling samples, it is essential to keep the sheets in consecutive order. This is best accomplished by stapling the sheets together when they are collected. The sheets should also be labeled according to position: the top sheet should be labeled "top #1,"

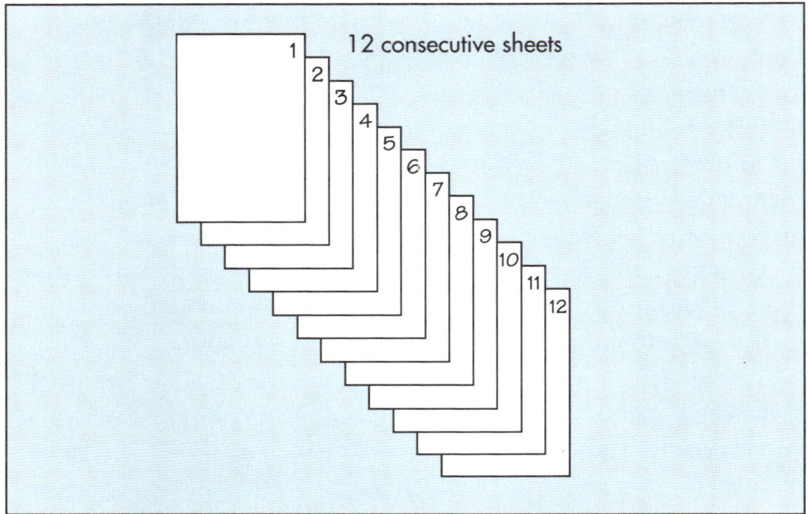

Collecting and keeping sheets in consecutive order is important for complaint analysis.

through to the bottom sheet, which would be labeled "bottom #12." Samples should include 12 consecutive sheets from the feeder and 12 consecutive sheets from the delivery, taken at the time the problem is occurring. The samples should show the problem, whether it is a printing problem, a curl problem, or a contamination problem. Immediately after the initial paper samples have been collected, labeled, and placed in the complaint box, paper from another order, or a competitive grade, should be run with the paper that is experiencing the problem. Again, samples should be saved, labeled, and placed in the complaint box and retained until the complaint has been resolved.

Ink samples from both the fountain and ink can should be placed in appropriate sample containers (small metal cans, not paper cups), and fountain solution from the fountain trays should be collected in watertight plastic containers. These samples should be labeled and added to the complaint box. The accurate and immediate labeling of samples is extremely important. Waiting too long to label the samples greatly increases the chances of mixing them up and is a significant cause of confusing information.

Another risky practice is pulling the defective job, and having to put it back on press to show the problem. Often the job will run just fine after being put back on press. It may well be that all of the marginal paper was used in "fighting" the problem, or it may have taken several impressions for the problem to show. It is not unusual for problematic interactions between paper, ink, and fountain solution to disappear or behave differently when the job is rerun, due to changes in temperature, ink, or length of run.

Debris

Particles causing blanket contamination such as surface debris, picking, pickouts, or contamination from other sources should be collected for microscopic and chemical analysis. These particles can be removed from the blanket with a knife and placed in a small closed container, or they may be removed with cellophane tape and mounted on a clean plastic sheet of acetate or Mylar. Never adhere the tape to itself or to paper. As particles are collected, identify and label the sample by the printing unit or units from which particles were taken. If possible, try to match one or more of these particles with the defect it created in the printed sheets by sorting through the printed pile to locate the original defect. Circle the defect, being sure to include the six sheets immediately preceding and the six sheets immediately following this sheet and marking their printing sequence. Staple one of their corners to keep them in proper sequence.

Collect twelve consecutive sheets of the unprinted paper. With a single pass, wipe across the edges of a lift of the unprinted paper with a black cloth. If there is a significant accumulation of white particles, enclose the cloth in an envelope as part of the evidence.

Blanket Piling

To report on blanket piling, state whether the piling is occurring in the image or nonimage areas, on which printing units it is occurring, and the color involved in the piling. If at all possible, remove the blanket showing the piling condition and retain it so that the paper supplier may examine it. Otherwise, collect some of the piled material by scraping it from the blanket and placing it in a small container, or remove the material with cellophane tape and mount it on a plastic sheet. If piling is occurring on more than one press unit, collect samples from each unit and immediately label the samples. A photograph of blanket piling after a stated number of impressions is helpful. Collect several press sheets and mark the areas where print quality has deteriorated due to piling. Indicate the number of impressions these sheets represent from the previous washup. A sample of fountain solution and ink from the fountains should be submitted as part of the supporting evidence.

Blistering

Evidence and information needed to support a blistering claim should include twelve consecutive printed sheets or signatures that illustrate blistering, the roll number, approximately 10 ft. (3 m) of the full roll width of the unprinted paper, the temperature of the web as it leaves the dryer, and the press speed. Be sure to immediately label the samples as they are being collected.

Curl

It is sometimes difficult to collect samples of curled paper and have them show the same condition of curl after they have been shipped to the paper supplier. Photographs of the paper before and after printing may best illustrate how a curl problem looked at the time of printing. These photographs can include the paper's labeling or identifying information. When samples of paper are shipped for evidence of curl, they must be shipped flat and be well-protected from bending. A newly opened carton or skid should be photographed immediately, as should paper that has been opened for a period of time. Information that needs to be reported about a curl problem includes the relative humidity and temperature of the pressroom at the time the curl occurred, the direction of the curl, whether the curl is to the felt or wire side, and whether it is across or with the grain direction. It is also important to know when the curl became evident—that is, before printing, after printing, when the first side was printed, or when the second side was printed.

Damaged Blankets

The folded or defective sheet or the material or object that caused blanket damage should be recovered and saved, along with the six printed sheets immediately preceding and the six printed sheets immediately following the printing impression at which damage occurred. The unwashed damaged blanket or blankets should be kept as part of the evidence, and the printing unit or units on which damage occurred should be noted.

Misregister and Wrinkles

For misregister and wrinkling problems related to paper, collect twelve consecutive press sheets and mark the areas containing the problem. If unprinted sheet paper has wavy or tight edges or some other visible distortion, take photographs illustrating its condition and collect twelve sheets of the unprinted paper. As soon as a new carton or skid of the same lot is opened, take photographs and collect twelve sheets to illustrate its condition.

For misregister and press wrinkling problems related to roll condition, take photographs of a laid-out, unwound strip from the roll or the web as it feeds into the press. This procedure will show uneven tension, bagginess, or other visible distortion. Collect twelve press sheets or signatures and mark the area that illustrates the problem. Take 6–8 ft. (2–3 m) of unprinted paper (full width) from the problem roll and mark the boundaries of areas that are baggy, slack, distorted, or otherwise believed to be causing the problem. Identify them by their roll number. Do not fold samples; ship them in a large-diameter mailing tube.

Low Printed Gloss and Mottle

Mark areas of the press sheet or signature to illustrate the problem. Collect the six sheets or signatures immediately preceding the sheet illustrating the problem and the six immediately following this marked sheet. Keep the sheets in sequence and number them "prior to the problem" and "after the problem." If the paper has not been backed up, back up 50–75 sheets and collect twelve consecutive sheets. This procedure will show whether only one side of the sheet has a mottle problem or whether mottle is common to both sides.

Identify the first sheets or, for a roll, 6–8 ft. (2–3 m) of the full roll width. In addition, for each printing unit, completely fill a small ink can with an ink sample, seal the can, and identify the ink by brand name and number.

Web Breaks

Web breaks are a serious problem for all forms of web printing and can occur anywhere on the press, from infeed to cutoff. Breaks result in costly downtime, paper waste, and, frequently, damage to printing plates and blankets. Excessive web tension contributes to web breaks by stretching the paper and reducing its resiliency. On the other hand, most papers have tensile strengths well in excess of the normal infeed tension used for web printing. It usually takes a local weakness or defect in the web, or excessive tension on its edge, to initiate a web break. Following are known causes of most web breaks with suggested preventive measures and remedies.

- Excessive tension on one or both edges of the web due to moisture loss and shrinking is making the web tight-edged and baggy. This condition can start tears at one or both edges and cause web breaks. Keeping rolls wrapped, making certain their wrappings are undamaged, and humidifying their storage area during winter are preventive steps.
- There is excessive tension on one edge of the web due to a tapered roll— that is, one having a nonuniform diameter. Sometimes turning the roll end-for-end will help this situation. Tapered rolls should be reported to the mill.
- A roll has a stuck or cracked edge or a dent, nick, or cut on its end. Any edge defect is a weak spot where a tear can start and produce a web break.

- There are wrinkles, slime spots, foam spots, bursts, calender cuts, blister cuts, fiber cuts, or hair cuts, all potential causes of web breaks. While these defects cannot be entirely avoided in paper manufacturing, their occurrence should be minimal.
- Bad mill splices can cause web breaks.
- An out-of-round, or wobbling, roll gives a jerky web infeed and subjects the web to sudden high tension.
- Faulty press alignment can cause web breaks.

A sample of each web break, including both ends of the break, should be collected and identified by its roll number and its position in the roll—that is, near the core, middle, or outer diameter part of the roll. Also record the location on press where the break occurred. Evidence of the manner in which breaks occur is helpful in determining and eliminating their causes.

Standard acceptable practice in the industry states that the printer is responsible for a certain number of breaks per 100 rolls, depending on the weight of the paper.

Claims for excessive web breaks for runs less than 100 rolls are negotiable. Web breaks beyond those listed are the responsibility of the mill if evidence is provided to support the claim.

Basis Weight of Paper	Number of Breaks
38 lb.	8
40 lb.	7
43–60 lb.	6
>60 lb.	5

Industry standard acceptable number of breaks per 100 rolls. (From The Paper Buyers' Encyclopedia)

11 Selecting Envelopes

There are envelopes to fit most any use: envelopes for coins, drugs, theater, security, business and personal correspondence, catalogs, and announcements. All envelopes that are used for mailing are subject to postal regulations, which require that envelopes be at least 3×4¼ in. (76×121 mm) and be square or rectangular. Because of the many sizes, styles, and design characteristics, it is always advisable to consult with merchants or manufacturers about available styles and their intended end-use. If special sizes are desired, they can be specially ordered on a "making order" basis. Keep in mind, however, that just as in making orders for paper, the cost and delivery time will increase.

Envelopes are classified as either open-end, with the opening on the short dimension, or open-sided, with the opening on the long dimension. They are identified by names such as *baronial, announcements, catalog, commercial, clasp,* and *string-and-button,* coming in various sizes depending on the intended use. Some envelopes may also be identified by number. A no. 10 commercial envelope, for example, is 4⅛×9½ in. (105×241 mm).

White envelopes are usually made from 20-, 24-, or 28-lb. bond paper, while envelopes that require strength are made from brown kraft paper. Envelopes made from 20-lb. bond will have less opacity than those made from 24- or 28-lb. bond.

Merchant catalogs are readily available and should be used as a source of information. An example of a typical listing in a merchant's pricing book for no. 10 commercial envelopes, measuring 4⅛×9½ in., is shown on the next page.

Item	Envelope #	Sub	Ctn Pkg	Number of cartons <1	1	5	10	20	40
Merchant Catalog #	10	24	5000	*Price per 1000 envelopes*					

A typical listing in a merchant's pricing book, showing price brackets.

In the above example, only its number (no. 10) identifies the envelope. "Sub" is short for substance, referring to the basis weight of the paper from which the envelopes were made. In the above example, *Sub 24* indicates 24-lb. bond paper. "Ctn Pkg" (carton package) indicates the number of envelopes in a carton; in the above example there are 5000. Envelopes, like paper, have price breaks based on the number ordered. For commercial envelopes those breaks occur at less than a carton, 1 carton, 5 cartons, 10 cartons, 20 cartons, and 40 cartons. Always check with the supplier to be sure of price brackets.

ENVELOPE STYLES

Some of the more popular envelopes are listed below with information on their use, style, and size range. A complete list of envelope sizes and styles can be found in the envelope section of *The Paper Buyers' Encyclopedia* or in merchant paper catalogs and price books.

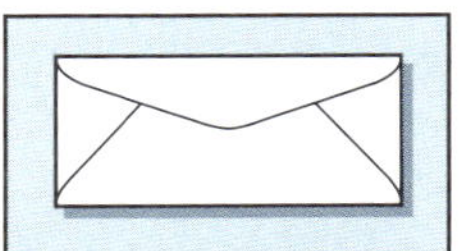

Commercial envelopes are produced in both kraft and bond papers. This envelope is used mostly for business and personal correspondence such as letters, statements, direct mailing and invoices. Sizes range from 3⁵⁄₁₆×5½ in. (78×140 mm) [no. 5], to 5×11½ in. (127×292 mm) [no. 14].

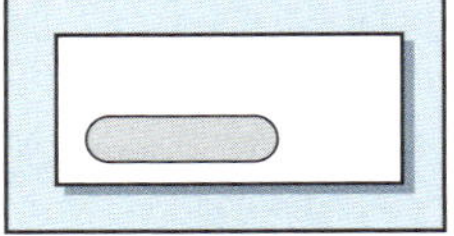

Window envelopes are used mainly for invoices, dividends, and statements. They are available in white or color. Some are tinted inside. Sizes range from 3½×6 in. (311×152 mm) [no. 6¼] to 3⅞×7½ in. (98×191 mm) [no. 7¾].

Self-sealing envelopes are produced with latex adhesive on upper and lower flaps that seal without moisture and save time in handling. The sizes for this style of envelope are limited. *The Paper Buyer's Encyclopedia, 22nd edition,* lists only two sizes: $3\frac{5}{8}$×$6\frac{1}{2}$ in. (92×165 mm) [no. $6\frac{3}{4}$] and $4\frac{1}{2}$×$9\frac{1}{2}$ in. (114×241 mm) [no. 10].

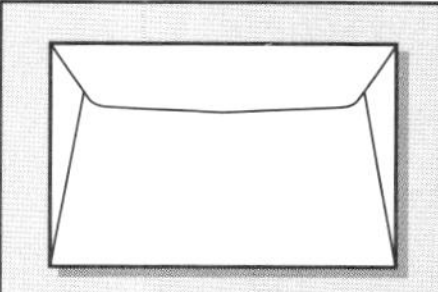

Booklet (open-side) envelopes are ideal for direct mailings, annual reports, brochures, and in-house correspondence. They lend themselves to overall printing, front and back, due to a concealed seam. Sizes range from $3\frac{1}{4}$×$6\frac{3}{4}$ in. (83×171 mm) [no. 1] to $9\frac{1}{2}$×$12\frac{5}{8}$ (241×321 mm) [no. 10].

Baronial envelopes are formal open-sided envelopes with deep, pointed flaps. They are often used for greeting cards, announcements, and invitations. Sizes range from $3\frac{5}{8}$×$5\frac{1}{8}$ in. (92×130 mm) [no. 4] to 5×$6\frac{1}{4}$ in. (127×159 mm) [no. 6].

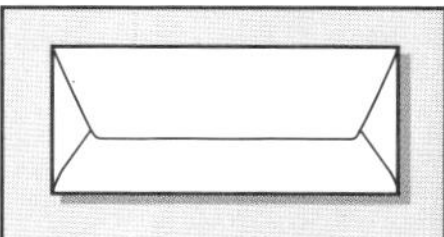

Banker's flap and wallet flap envelopes are far stronger than normal commercial envelopes, and they can handle a large volume of material safely. Sizes range from $3\frac{7}{8}$×$7\frac{1}{2}$ in. (98×191 mm) [no. $7\frac{3}{4}$] to 6×12 in. (152×305 mm) [no. 16].

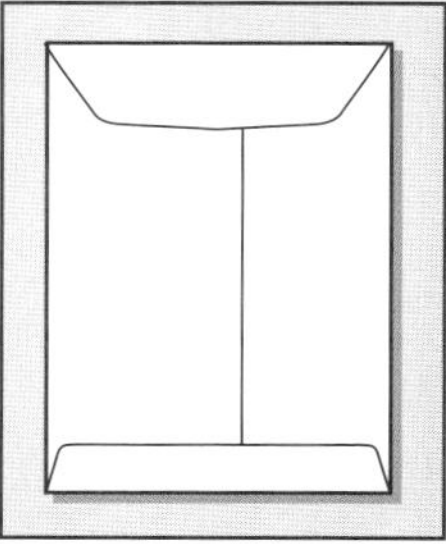

Catalog (open-end) envelopes are used for mailing booklets, magazines, catalogs, and reports. With their wide seams and heavy gummed flaps, they offer ideal protection for enclosed material. Sizes range from 4×$6\frac{3}{8}$ in. (102×162 mm) [no. 7] to 12×$15\frac{1}{2}$ in. (305×394 mm) [no. $15\frac{1}{2}$].

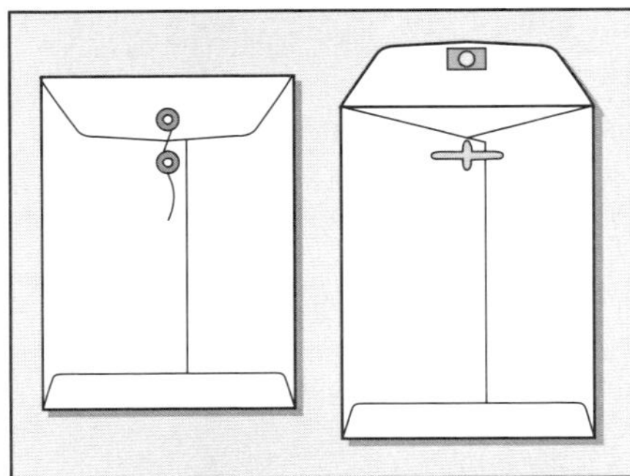

String-and-button and clasp envelopes are able to be opened and closed many times. They are widely used, due to their sturdiness, for mailing bulky papers or brochures. These envelopes are usually available in brown or gray kraft. Sizes range from 3⅛×5½ in. (79×140 mm) [no. 5] to 12×15½ in. (305×394 mm) [no. 110].

Expansion envelopes are designed to hold bulky material. The fully expanded sizes range from 4½×11×1⅛ in. (114×279×29 mm) to 9×12×3 in. (229×305×76 mm).

Glossary

Absolute humidity The total amount of water vapor in a unit volume of the atmosphere.

Adhesive-coated paper Paper coated on one side with an adhesive that is activated by moistening (for gummed papers) or by heat (for heat-sealing) or that is permanently tacky (for pressure-sensitive applications).

Antique A paper finish, typically found in book paper and cover paper, characterized by a rough surface intended to simulate old, handmade paper.

Artificial parchment A paper, resembling genuine vegetable parchment, produced from a wildly formed fibrous structure.

Basic size The adopted sheet size used to define basis weight, differing for various papers. See *basis weight.*

Basis weight The weight in pounds per ream of paper cut to its basic size in inches.

Blanket In lithography, a rubber-coated fabric mounted on a cylinder that receives the inked impression from the plate and transfers (or offsets) it to the paper.

Brightness (1) The subjective perception of luminous intensity from any light sensation, running the gamut from lightness and brilliance to dimness or darkness. (2) With paper, the percent reflectance of blue light only, centering on the wavelength of 457 nm.

Bulk The thickness of a pile of an exact number of sheets of paper under a specified pressure.

Business forms bond A bond paper manufactured for the specific requirements of web printing and converting, and the end-uses of continuous business forms.

Calendering Passing the web between the nips of steel rolls at the end of the paper machine to impart the desired finish.

Caliper The thickness of a single sheet of paper or the perpendicular distance between two surfaces, as measured with a micrometer that applies a static load for a specific time; expressed as points, or thousandths of an inch, in traditional units and in micrometers in metric units.

Carbonless paper Paper that uses a chemical reaction between two different contacting coatings to transfer images when pressure is applied.

Cast-coated A high-gloss, ink-absorbent paper with an enamel finish. Cast-coated paper is dried under pressure against a polished cylinder during manufacture.

Cockle (1) The effect of uneven moisture absorption on paper. The paper swells in the areas of greatest absorption, which causes a slightly bumpy surface contour. (2) A finish produced by air-drying bond and onionskin papers.

COLOR BARS A device printed in a trim area of a press sheet to monitor printing variables such as trapping, ink density, dot gain, and print contrast. It usually consists of overprints of two- and three-color solids and tints; solid and tint blocks of cyan, magenta, yellow, and black; and additional aids such as resolution targets and dot gain scales. Alternative terms: *color control strip; color control bar.*

COVER PAPER A heavy paper designed to serve as the outer layer and protective cover of a booklet or paper application.

CROSS-MACHINE DIRECTION A direction perpendicular to the direction of web travel through the paper machine.

DANDY ROLL A hollow wire-covered roll that rides on the paper machine wire and compacts the wet, newly formed web to improve its formation and, if required, impart a watermark or laid finish to the paper.

DECKLE EDGE The untrimmed feather edge of paper produced at the edges of the web on the paper machine. Deckle edges are sometimes artificially produced.

DEW POINT The temperature at which air of a given absolute humidity becomes saturated with water vapor.

DIMENSIONAL STABILITY The degree to which paper maintains its linear dimensions with changes in its moisture content or applied stresses.

DULL FINISH ENAMEL An enamel paper that is supercalendered to low gloss level.

EMBOSSED FINISH A surface pattern given to paper by passing a web between the nip of an engraved metal roll and a matching soft backing roll.

EQUILIBRIUM MOISTURE CONTENT The moisture content of paper having the same relative humidity as its surrounding atmosphere, under which condition the paper neither loses nor gains moisture when exposed to the atmosphere.

FELT FINISH A finish applied to paper at the wet press with felts having a weave different from that of normal paper machine felts.

FELT SIDE The top side of paper formed on the single-wire paper machine.

FINISH The surface characteristics of paper, often described by a single term such as vellum or wove.

FLEXOGRAPHY A method of rotary letterpress printing characterized by the use of flexible rubber or plastic plates with raised image areas and fluid, rapid-drying inks. Alternative term: *aniline printing.*

FOUNTAIN SOLUTION In lithographic printing, a combination of water, gum arabic, and other chemicals used to wet the printing plate and keep the nonimage areas from accepting ink. Some fountain solutions contain alcohol. Alternative term: *dampening solution.*

FOUR-COLOR PROCESS PRINTING The photomechanical reproduction of multicolor images achieved by overprinting specified amounts and areas of yellow, cyan, magenta, and black inks.

GLOSS The attribute of paper that causes it to be shiny or lustrous.

GRAIN The pronounced alignment of paper fibers in the direction of their flow on the paper machine.

GRAIN-LONG Having grain parallel to the longer dimension of the sheet.

GRAIN-SHORT Having grain parallel to the shorter dimension of the sheet.

GRAMMAGE The designation of paper or paperboard weight in the metric system as grams per square meter.

GROUNDWOOD PULP Pulp produced by grinding bark-free logs against a revolving stone in the presence of water at atmospheric pressure.

GUMMED PAPER A paper coated on one side with an adhesive activated by water.

HAIR CUT A smooth, curved cutting of the web that occurs as an imbedded hair passes through the calender.

HARDNESS The degree of a paper's resistance to indentation by some other material or object, such as type, a printing plate, or a stylus, pen, or pencil.

HEAT-RESISTANT SPLICE A splice made with splicing materials that will not soften and cause splice failure when the paper web reaches elevated temperatures during heatset drying.

HEAT-SEAL PAPER A label coated on one side with an adhesive that is activated and becomes tacky with the application of heat.

HEATSET PRINTING A method of printing, usually by web offset, in which the inks dry by passing the printed paper web through a hot-air dryer at a temperature of 250–500°F (120–250°C) and then cooling it to 75–90°F (24–32°C) by passing the web over a series of chill rolls that reduce the temperature of the inks below their setting point.

HUMIDITY A term that describes the presence and quantity of water vapor existing as a gas along with other gases in the atmosphere.

HYGROMETER An instrument used to measure the relative humidity of air.

HUE The primary and most basic attribute of a color that makes it distinct from another color, determined by its dominant wavelength of light on the visible spectrum. In ink manufacturing and color matching, hue is more commonly known as shade.

INDEX BRISTOL A bristol paper designed for file cards and records, index systems, and ruled forms.

INK ABSORBENCY The property of paper that determines the rate and the amount of ink penetration into its surface after ink is applied by the press plate or blanket.

INK HOLDOUT The extent to which paper retards the inward penetration of a freshly printed ink film.

INKJET PRINTING A nonimpact printing process that produces images on paper by electrically controlling the flow of a high-velocity stream of microscopic ink droplets from a pressurized inkjet system.

INK RECEPTIVITY The ability of a paper surface to accept ink uniformly and adequately from the plate or blanket during printing.

KRAFT PAPER A strong paper made from sulfate pulp, used for products like wrapping, bags, and envelopes.

LABEL PAPER A paper, usually coated on one side, made for the specific requirements of labeling applications, including printing, finishing, and performance with labeling equipment.

LAID FINISH A finish produced with a dandy roll having closely spaced wires.

LATEX-TREATED PAPER Paper whose fibrous network is impregnated with latex for durability, high edge-tear resistance, wet strength, and flexible, leatherlike properties. It may be coated for improved printability and resistance to oils, grease, and water.

LEDGER PAPER A paper similar to bond, but made in heavier basis weights to provide the stiffness and durability needed for data entry, ruling, and record systems.

"M" WEIGHT The weight of 1,000 sheets of paper in a specific basic size.

MACHINE DIRECTION The direction in which fibers flow to the paper machine; the direction of web travel through the paper machine.

MACHINE FINISH A smooth finish obtained on the paper machine by calendering.

MAKING ORDER An order for items not stocked but made according to the specifications of the purchaser.

MANIFOLD PAPER A lightweight bond paper used for making carbon or manifold copies or for airmail correspondence.

MATTE SURFACE A surface having a very low gloss, reflecting most of the incident light in all directions.

MICR CHECK PAPER Paper suitable for checks whose characters are printed with magnetic ink in a special magnetic ink character recognition font that permits automatic sorting and processing by special equipment.

MOISTURE-BARRIER WRAPPER A wrapper designed to act as a barrier to the transmission of moisture, to prevent the harmful consequences of moisture loss or gain.

MOISTURE CONTENT The amount of moisture contained by paper, expressed as a percentage of its total weight.

MOTTLED Visibly nonuniform density, gloss, or color of printed ink films. Alternative term: *galvanized.*

NEWSPRINT A paper manufactured mostly from groundwood or mechanical pulp, specifically for printing newspapers.

NIP The line of contact between two rolls in a papermaking or printing operation, particularly those through which the paper passes (such as a calender, supercalender, or offset printing press).

NONRETURNABLE CORE A fiber or paper roll core that is used only once.

OFFSET PAPER A printing paper, coated or uncoated, made for the specific requirements of offset printing.

ONIONSKIN A lightweight, air-dried, cockle finish bond paper used for file copies of correspondence and for airmail stationery.

OPACITY The property of paper that obstructs its light transmission and prevents the show-through of printing.

OUT-OF-ROUNDNESS A roll shape irregularity caused by storing a roll on its side, using excessive roll clamp pressure, or dropping or bumping the roll.

OUT-TURNED SAMPLE A representative sample taken from a run of paper or from a delivery.

PAPERBOARD A paperlike product having greater basis weight, thickness, and rigidity than paper. With a few exceptions, paperboard has a thickness of 12 points (0.3 mm) or more.

PICKING A disruption of a paper surface strong enough to overcome the internal bonding of the fibers or of the coating to the base paper. Picking is caused by tack forces of the ink and rubber blanket. Alternative term: *plucking.*

PILING Materials from paper, ink, or paper and ink that accumulate on a blanket in sufficient quantity to affect print quality. Piling may occur in the image or nonimage areas.

PLY (1) A designation of thickness for blanks and other paperboards. (2) The number of individual sheets of paper that make up a set of business forms.

PRESS GRIPPER The metal clamps and fingers, located on impression cylinders and transfers cylinders of a sheetfed printing press, that grasp and hold a sheet of paper while it is being transported through the press.

PRINT QUALITY The degree to which the appearance and other properties of a print approach the desired result.

PULP Fibrous material for papermaking produced either mechanically or chemically from cellulose raw material.

REAM A standard count designation for 500 sheets of paper.

REAM WEIGHT The weight, in pounds, of one ream of paper.

REGISTER The overall agreement in the position of printing detail on a press sheet, especially the alignment of two or more overprinted colors in multicolor presswork. Register may be observed by agreement of overprinted register marks on a press sheet. In stripping, film flats are usually punched and held together with pins to ensure register. The punched holes on the film flat match those on the plate and press specified for the job. Alternative term: *registration.*

RELATIVE HUMIDITY The percent ratio of the pressure of water vapor in the air to the pressure of the saturated water vapor in air at the same temperature; the percent ratio of the amount of water vapor in the air to the maximum amount the air can hold at the same temperature.

RIGIDITY Resistance to bending or flexing.

ROTOGRAVURE A printing process that uses a cylinder as an image carrier. Image areas are etched below nonimage areas in the form of tiny sunken cells. The cylinder is immersed in ink, and the excess ink is scraped off by a blade. When the substrate contacts the printing cylinder, ink transfers, forming the image.

RUNNABILITY The ability of a paper to be printed without causing problems in the mechanics of the printing operation.

SATURATED AIR Air that contains the maximum amount of water vapor it can hold at its existing temperature; air whose relative humidity is 100%.

SHOW-THROUGH Visibility of printing on the reverse side of the paper.

SIZING The treatment of paper with materials or chemicals to impart resistance to water, oils, and other fluids, to seal down its surface fibers, and to improve its surface strength.

SLIME SPOT A fragile spot or hole in the paper resulting from a bacterial growth or slime that originated in the papermaking system and was formed into the paper.

SLING PSYCHROMETER A device having wet- and dry-bulb thermometers that are whirled vertically in the atmosphere to provide readings from which, in conjunction with psychrometric tables, the percent relative humidity is determined.

SPLICING On a web press, the process of joining the web lead of a new paper roll to the end of the expiring roll, to permit continuous running of the press.

STANDARD SIZE Full-size sheets of paper, representing the sizes most commonly used and differing for different grades of paper.

STIFFNESS The ability of paper or paperboard to resist an applied bending force; especially, its ability to support its own weight when handled.

SULFATE PULP Chemical pulp produced by cooking wood chips in a solution of sodium hydroxide and sodium sulfide.

SULFITE PULP Chemical pulp produced by cooking wood chips with sulfurous acid and one of its base salts, which may be calcium, sodium, magnesium, or ammonia.

SUPERCALENDER A calender consisting of alternate hard steel rolls and soft filled rolls, giving a high-gloss finish to paper passing through the nips because of slippage that occurs between a hard and soft roll. A supercalender is operated separately from a paper machine or coater.

TACK The resistance of an ink film to being split between to surfaces, as between rollers, plate and blanket, or blanket and paper.

TAG A strong, dense, hard, heavily calendered paper made from sulfate pulp and used for heavy-duty applications.

TAPPI BRIGHTNESS The reflecting power of a pad of paper as measured with blue light (457 nm) under prescribed optical and geometrical conditions, as described in the TAPPI Official Test Method T 452.

TECHNICAL ASSOCIATION OF THE PULP AND PAPER INDUSTRY (TAPPI) A professional organization having international membership among the paper and allied industries, whose purpose is to further scientific advancement, research, and technical manpower needs, and to establish recognized technical standards (TAPPI Standards) and testing procedures pertaining to the manufacture and use of pulp and paper.

TEMPERATURE CONDITIONING Bringing paper to pressroom temperature before it is unwrapped and printed.

TEXT PAPER Fine-quality printing paper available in many finishes and textured surfaces, in white and colors, and with plain or deckle edges. Text is designed for deluxe printed booklets, programs, announcements, and advertising, and may be watermarked.

TIGHT EDGES Paper edges that have lost moisture and have shrunk because of their exposure to an atmosphere having a lower relative humidity than that of the paper.

TRIM (1) The widest web of paper, after allowance for trimmed edges, that can be made on a paper machine. (2) The paper trimmed off the edges of a web or sheet during finishing.

TWO-SIDEDNESS A paper property that describes the difference in texture, appearance, and printability between the side of the paper formed in contact with the papermaking machine's forming wire (the wire side) and that which is formed on the top, away from the forming wire (the felt side).

UNDERRUN The production and delivery of paper in less than the quantity ordered.

VEGETABLE PARCHMENT A greaseproof paper with high wet strength, made by passing a paper web through a sulfuric acid bath that fuses its fibers into a homogenous mass.

VELLUM FINISH A fine-grained paper finish, smoother than antique.

WATERMARK A localized modification in a sheet of paper, usually consisting of a visible reduction in the opacity of the paper, resulting in a translucent image. A watermark is produced by a dandy roll or watermarking bands while the paper still contains a large amount of water.

WAVY EDGES Edges of paper that have become wavy and distorted by moisture absorption and fiber expansion due to exposure to a higher relative humidity than that of the paper or from cold paper being unwrapped and exposed to warmer air.

WEB A roll of any substrate that passes continuously through a printing press or converting or finishing equipment.

WEB DRYER A hot-air unit on a web press that warms up the printed web to evaporate the solvents in the heatset ink. The web then passes over a series of large-diameter cylinders, called chill rolls, that reduce the temperature of the inks to their setting point.

WEB OFFSET A lithographic printing process in which a press prints on a continuous roll of paper instead of individual sheets.

WEDDING PAPER A paper having a very uniform, closed formation and a refined surface without glare, used for printed and engraved wedding stationery, announcements, and executive correspondence.

WHITENESS The extent to which paper diffusely reflects light of all wavelengths throughout the visible spectrum. The assigned ideal white standard totally reflects all light throughout the spectrum.

WIRE SIDE The side of the paper formed by contact with the paper machine wire.

WORK-AND-TUMBLE IMPOSITION An imposition that uses the same guide edge of the press sheet and press guide but a different gripper edge of the sheet for printing its second side. Alternative term: *work-and-flop imposition.*

WORK-AND-TURN IMPOSITION An imposition that uses the same gripper edge of the press sheet but the opposite press guide for printing its second side. Alternative term: *print-and-turn imposition.*

WOVE FINISH Having the normal or regular finish of paper, as produced with a plain-woven wire covering on the dandy roll.

INDEX

About the Author

Larry Wilson is president of Wilson's Consulting Service, Arrowsic, Maine. He is the author of *What the Printer Should about Paper,* published by GATF*Press* and available in English and Spanish.

A graduate of the Rochester Institute of Technology with degrees in printing and chemistry, he started his career in graphic arts as superintendent of W.B. Saunders Publishing Company's offset printing plant, where he worked for six years. For the next 30 years Wilson worked for S.D Warren Company, a major paper manufacturer, where he handled customer complaints and directed the company's graphic arts research efforts. He spent the last ten years of his career with S.D. Warren as a leader for total quality management (TQM) and as human resource director.

Wilson also headed the Graphic Communications Association (GCA) Print Properties Committee. This committee, under his leadership, tested all phases of the printing process affecting image reproduction and quality. He has twenty-five years of professional and academic experience as an art director, teacher, and consultant in visual communication, multimedia, and graphics technology, working with both small and Fortune 500 companies. His designs have been reproduced in various graphic journals and used for more than one hundred publications in the U.S. and abroad. He also has written a series of articles on the subjects of visual communication.

About GATF

The Graphic Arts Technical Foundation is a nonprofit, scientific, technical, and educational organization dedicated to the advancement of the graphic communications industries worldwide. Its mission is to serve the field as the leading resource for technical information and services through research and education. GATF is a partner of the Printing Industries of America (PIA), the world's largest graphic arts trade association, and its regional affiliates.

For 77 years the Foundation has developed leading edge technologies and practices for printing. GATF's staff of researchers, educators, and technical specialists partner with nearly 14,000 corporate members in over 80 countries to help them maintain their competitive edge by increasing productivity, print quality, process control, and environmental compliance, and by implementing new techniques and technologies. Through conferences, satellite symposia, workshops, consulting, technical support, laboratory services, and publications, GATF strives to advance a global graphic communications community.

The Foundation publishes books on nearly every aspect of the field; learning modules (step-by-step instruction booklets); audiovisuals (CD-ROMs and videocassettes); and research and technology reports. It also publishes *GATFWorld,* a bimonthly magazine of technical articles, industry news, and reviews of specific products.

For detailed information about GATF products and services, please visit our website at *www.gatf.org* or *www.gain.net* or write to us at 200 Deer Run Road, Sewickley, PA 15143-2600. Phone: 412/741-6860. GATF and PIA publications may also be ordered online through the Graphic Arts Information Network at *www.gain.net.*

About PIA

In continuous operation since 1887 and headquartered in Alexandria, Virginia, Printing Industries of America, Inc. (PIA), is the world's largest graphic art trade association representing an industry with more than 1 million employees and $156 billion in sales annually. PIA promotes the interests of over 14,000 member companies. Companies become members in PIA by joining one of 30 regional affiliate organizations throughout the United States or by joining the Canadian Printing Industries Association. International companies outside North America may join PIA directly.

Printing Industries of America, Inc. is in the business of promoting programs, services, and an environment that helps its members operate profitably. Many of PIA's members are commercial printers, allied graphic arts firms such as electronic imaging companies, equipment manufacturers, and suppliers.

PIA has developed several special industry groups to meet the unique needs of specific market segments. Each special industry group provides members with current information on their specific market and helps members stay ahead of the competition. PIA's special industry groups are the Web Offset Association (WOA), Web Printing Association (WPA), Graphic Arts Marketing Information Service (GAMIS), International Thermographers Association (ITA), Label Printing Industries of America (LPIA), and Binding Industries of America International (BIA).

For more detailed information on PIA products and services, please visit our website *www.gain.net* or write to 100 Daingerfield Road, Alexandria, VA 22314 (phone: 703/519-8100).

GATF*Press*: Selected Titles

- ***Practical Proofreading***
  by Matthew Willen
- ***Printing Estimating Primer***
  Don Merit
- ***Glossary of Graphic Communications***
  compiled by Pamela Groff
- ***Understanding Graphic Communication***
  by Harvey Robert Levenson, Ph.D.
- ***Handbook of Printing Processes***
  by Deborah Stevenson
- ***Flexography Primer***
  by J. Page Crouch
- ***Gravure Primer***
  by Cheryl Kasunich
- ***Lithography Primer***
  by Dan Wilson
- ***On-Demand & Digital Printing Primer***
  by Howard M. Fenton
- ***The GATF Encyclopedia of Graphic Communications***
  by Frank Romano and Richard Romano
- ***Handbook of Graphic Arts Equations***
  by Manfred H. Breede
- ***Screen Printing Primer***
  by Samuel Ingram
- ***What the Printer Should Know About Paper***
  by Lawrence A. Wilson

Colophon

This first edition of *Paper Buying Primer* was edited, designed, and printed at the Graphic Arts Technical Foundation, headquartered in Sewickley, Pennsylvania. The text was created by the author using Microsoft Word, then edited at GATF and imported into QuarkXPress 4.0 on an Apple Power Macintosh. The primary fonts used for the interior of the book are New Baskerville and Futura. Illustrations were created using Adobe Illustrator 8.0. Pages were proofed on a Xerox Regal color copier with Splash RIP.

Once the editorial/page layout process was completed, the images were transmitted to GATF's Robert Howard Center for Imaging Excellence, where all images were adjusted for the printing parameters of GATF's in-house printing department and proofed.

After the book was preflighted using a Power Macintosh, Agfa's Apogee Series2 PDF production system was used to impose the pages, and then the book was output to a Creo Trendsetter 3244 platesetter. The interior of the book was printed as 16- and 32-page signatures on GATF's 26×40-in., four-color Heidelberg Speedmaster Model 102-4P sheetfed perfecting press, and the cover was printed four-up on GATF's 20×28-in., six-color Komori Lithrone 28 sheetfed press with tower coater. Finally, the book was sent to a trade bindery for perfect binding.